LIVING
WITH
BROKEN
GLASS

The Gifts of Grief

LIVING
WITH
BROKEN
GLASS

The Gifts of Grief

SHELLY M ROWLAN

CFI
An imprint of Cedar Fort, Inc.
Springville, Utah

Paperback ISBN 13: 978-1-4621-4587-4
Ebook ISBN 13: 978-1-4621-4658-1

Published by CFI, an imprint of Cedar Fort, Inc.
2373 W. 700 S., Suite 100, Springville, UT 84663
Distributed by Cedar Fort, Inc., www.cedarfort.com

Library of Congress Registration Number: 2023942327

Cover design by Nada Orlic
Cover design © 2023 Cedar Fort, Inc.

Printed in the United States of America

10 9 8 7 6 5 4 3 2 1

Printed on acid-free paper

Dedicated to my husband, Stacey.

You won't find him mentioned much in this book, but every page—every moment—included him. Just know he was part of it all, long before anyone else knew and long after everyone else had forgotten.

Contents

Preface

ON SEPTEMBER 29, 2014, MY FRIEND PAM'S SON, RYAN, TOOK HIS own life. I knew Pam. I knew Ryan. I knew their entire family. Ryan had even taken our daughter to prom. But after this tragedy, I was so afraid that I would do something wrong that I did nothing at all. I thought about them and I felt for them, but I could not bring myself to express it to them. My husband went to visit them. I stayed home. I was worried I wouldn't have the inner resources to engage with their pain, so I stayed away.

Two and a half years later, on March 23, 2017, my son Brieson took his own life. I was astounded by the things people did for us.

Eight months later, my friend Trudi's son, Cameron, died unexpectedly. Trudi and I had been friends since her pregnancy with Cameron. As soon as this happened, people started calling me and asking me about Trudi and what they could do for her. Apparently, people expected me to be an experienced consultant on mourning, if not an expert.

That is when this book began in earnest. Even though I had written almost daily since Brieson's death, I had not thought I would share much about it. Grief is an incredibly private and intense period of time. Usually, the more I feel about something, the less I speak of it.

The following pages are the compilation of things I've learned and experienced. I assume some experiences will be universal and some will be unique, but either way, I can testify from hundreds of encounters that God is not being metaphorical when He says, "I will . . . ease the burdens which are put upon your shoulders, that even you cannot feel them upon your backs, even while you are in bondage, and this will I do that ye may stand as witnesses for me hereafter, and that ye

1

may know of a surety that I, the Lord God, do visit my people in their afflictions" (Mosiah 24:14).

This is my witness.

A Few Weeks In: My Glass

I WROTE THE FOLLOWING ABOUT THREE WEEKS AFTER MY SON DIED:

Almost everyone asks how I am doing. I am doing well—and that's the truth.

Ninety percent of the time I feel just like I always did—an ordinary person, living an ordinary life, doing ordinary things. But the rest of the time—the other ten percent—I feel as if I have swallowed a large piece of jagged glass.

And there is no way to *ever* get it out.

And . . . maybe I don't want to get it out because it's valuable to me—it awakens things inside of me.

Like tonight—it's 1:30 in the morning and I am lying here with my piece of glass. But I am not thinking about Brieson. I am thinking about *you*—all of *you*. All the people who reached out to us. All the people who ran (ran!) to us and who did so, so many things. Those very things that you might have felt were insufficient or awkwardly offered are the very things that rise up and get me through these dark moments—the moments you will never see.

I said that I feel just like I always did, but that is perhaps not quite accurate. Because I carry glass around inside of me now, I can never be the same person I was. But instead of creating scars, instead of wounding me, tonight I realize this glass may actually be illuminating. Tonight I see you as I never have before—your goodness, your radiance, the gift *you* are to me.

You are magnified in my eyes—because of the broken glass.

I thought this would be a fleeting illumination and analogy, but as the days and even years went by, this jagged glass, while certainly painful at times, provided countless moments of insight and consolation. The glass could transform into a window, a mirror, a lens, a telescope, an optic fiber, or dozens of other translucent things providing new perspectives on simple moments. The strangest events would ignite my glass, letting me know there was a lesson to learn. A great deal of these events were unknowingly instigated by the people around me.

Sometimes it was hard to believe all the ideas this glass presented, and I would push back against them. But the glass never accepted my earthly reasoning. And why should it? It wasn't part of this sphere—it operated on truths from other realms.

I'm not sure why this jagged glass started revealing so much to me; it would have been easy for it to have kept its secrets. Instead, it became a constant source of understanding principles and promises, and it illuminated miracle after miracle. That might sound completely wrong to you: miracles don't come from tragedies, miracles *prevent* tragedies, right?

I once thought the same.

Looking Back: Miracles

THIS JAGGED GLASS MOST OFTEN PERFORMED AS A MAGNIFIER, EN-larging and redefining small moments and directing me where to put my attention—because what I paid attention to drove my mood and behavior. I learned that believing *is* seeing, and attention *is* an act of believing. If I wanted joy, fulfillment, and love, then I had to look for those things in my life. This did not cause the bad things to go away, but it certainly mitigated their power over me.

Our culture makes it very easy to focus on the negative aspects of death. In fact, it's almost an expectation that we will do so. People seem to believe that in the days, weeks, and months following death, one must walk around with a gloomy aura, covered by clouds of de-spondency. This was certainly my expectation, though I couldn't ar-ticulate it at the time. But it didn't turn out to be the case, at least not all the time. If I put my effort toward seeing the good, then amaz-ing things revealed themselves and my life seemed purer, cleaner, and more meaningful than it ever had before.

I am fully aware that positive thinking will not change the past. I am not advocating that we pretend bad things never happen. Obviously, they do. Instead, I am coming to understand the gift of faith. I once thought that if I had enough faith, then my will would be done. Now I know that faith in Jesus Christ is just that: believing that *His* will is the best thing to be done.

I also have wondered about the purpose of this experience. But the longer the days go by, the more I realize it was so I could be a witness—a witness of so many things, especially of miracles. You may say, "But you didn't get your miracle—your son died." And I agree that his healed life would definitely be the big miracle I wanted. But instead, God told me to trust Him and sent people to help me heal.

Also, it could be that God *did* save my son's life—for years—and I just never really acknowledged those miraculous interventions because I was getting what I wanted. Instead, it was when I experienced a great loss, when I didn't get what I wanted, that I began to see the hand of God more clearly.

Let me explain what I mean by miracles. I know that people often use the word *miracle* to talk about common things that we should appreciate more. Things like butterflies are a miracle, or a beautiful sunset or even majestic mountains. Those are things that everyone comfortably acknowledges, "Yes, it's a miracle." But that's not the kind of miracle I'm talking about here. I'm talking about the kinds of miracles that upset people. I'm talking about the raw, heart-clutching kind of moments that no one likes to encounter because they require so much anguish before they arrive.

I have heard people say, "I am praying for a miracle." I guess they are assuming that miracles are easy answers. But I have found, after receiving hundreds (yes, hundreds) of miracles over the last several years, that real miracles require a great deal of fortitude.

If you want some reference points for this, look in the Bible. Almost every miracle Jesus performed was met with some sort of pushback. Although miracles bring benefit, you have to hold on to them despite the responses of negativity, disbelief, and mockery from the evidence-seekers. They want to know in what manner, to what degree, and under what conditions. Science seeks for repeatable data as validation, but miracles by their very nature are singular and exclusive. And therein lies the divergence between belief and proof. (For one of the best examples, see the story of the man born blind in John 9.)

Real miracles have consequences. Real miracles bring their own set of challenges. Real miracles aren't obvious to the whole world—just to a small set of believers. I am trusting that you are within this small set of believers.

Miracles aren't easily accepted by those who watch from the sidelines. In fact, usually bystanders try to explain them away or argue them into commonalities or natural explanations. But you know they are divine messages. You just know.

You might think you want an immediate healing like the woman who merely touched the fringe of Jesus' garment, but then you conveniently forget the fourteen years of affliction that preceded it. These moments that precede some miracles are filled with a kind of a desperation that reaches right down and rips out your heartstrings. Miracles aren't the easy answers that most people seem to believe they are. They require faith both before and after they occur. Real miracles are quite disruptive, both before and after they occur.

I assume some of these accounts (or maybe all) will make many readers uncomfortable, but I am going to recount them anyway—because they really happened. If you aren't a believer in miracles, then you probably want to set this aside right now; it will be a mind-battling read for you.

Almost eighteen months after Brieson's death, someone asked me, "Did you ever find out why he killed himself?"

I replied with the truth: "No. And I doubt I ever will." I guess to most people that must seem like a very difficult bridge to cross. Why did he do it? What sparked it?

I will never have that knowledge in this life—at least, I can't imagine how it would come. It will always be an unanswered question. But these moments, the ones I will recount in these pages, give me stability and peace and create an inner ballast. These ethereal experiences have a permanence to them. When I think on them, I feel safe and at peace. Maybe that feeling is just as important as apprehending a cause and effect.

I write this book with three purposes:

- To testify that God is always at work in our lives by recounting the tender mercies, miracles, and revelations that occurred.
- To provide understanding on how to mourn with those who mourn by describing the things others did.
- To honor those who gave so much to me. *You are the hero of this book.*

Describing spiritual and emotional things is difficult; there simply aren't enough adjectives and adverbs to describe some encounters. I have struggled with the descriptions, but I can assure you they are never exaggerated. They can't be. There is no adequate earthly language for heavenly manifestations.

I could have organized this into the three purposes above, but instead I mixed them all together because that's how they came—unexpectedly, in the tangle of my days. Sorting them out is a process I am not capable of doing. I will explain as best I can, but following the thread requires faith. I wish this story was a neatly packaged fictional account, but it is not—it is real and therefore doesn't have the all-knowing narrator effect. There will be some loose ends and weird twists that I can't explain, and my experiences don't tie up in a cute little bow at the end.

I am still right here in the trenches with you, and I still can't see the whole battle plan. But that doesn't mean I haven't had real experiences. They just won't all fold into the grand stratagem of a postwar saga. I am still in the battle and not fully sure how it will all end, but this is my current field report.

Keep in mind that this book is about the best moments—the gifting moments. But there were also lots of bad moments. I think you can easily conjecture those dark parts, but what I had never imagined—never even considered—was all the glitter that would float across the pitch black.

Day 0: Slips of Paper

ONLY GOD KNOWS WHEN A TEST WILL COME—A TEST THAT CHANGES the landscape of your interior forever. Mine came on a Thursday, an ordinary Thursday, and like all tragedies, it came without preamble and without warning. It was something I had never planned to experience, and yet in the strangest ways, I had been prepared.

In January, over two months prior to this particular Thursday, there was a Relief Society activity that entailed everyone writing one complimentary thing about every other person in the room. There were probably thirty women in attendance. They then compiled and distributed them. I received my collection of compliments, quickly read through them that night, and tossed them on my nightstand in a pile of other things.

Two months went by, and I would notice them occasionally while looking for other things. I wanted to glue an envelope with them into my monthly photo book as a kind of scrapbook-type insert, but despite moving them around several times a week, I never quite got around to doing it.

On March 23, 2017, I notice those loose slips of paper for about the hundredth time. I stop and gather them up. I sit on the floor next to my bed with my back to the door, and one by one, I start to read the complimentary things others had written about me.

As I hold each small slip of paper in my hand, slowly, almost imperceptibly, an impression settles over me. It's as if someone has entered the room behind me—a very strong presence of someone standing and watching, proudly smiling down on me behind my back. The sense of it is so strong that I actually turn around to see who is there.

No one. No one is there. I glance around the room—the entire room. No one. I turn back to the papers, and a feeling of gratitude begins to fill me like a hose plugged into my heart. Every slip of paper twists the spout further open.

Perhaps you think I have incredible attributes or that the slips of paper are eloquently written, but they say very little compared to the emotional response they instigate. I am taken by surprise at the powerful feelings that accompany each brief compliment. I slowly consider each one as I read it, refold it, and then slide it into the glassine envelope.

I then carefully glue the envelope into the photo book, pressing down to secure it. All the while, the space around me seems to be filling up, crowding together.

Wanting to get this completed, I take the book and start up the two flights of stairs to place it on the library shelf with the others. As I turn onto the first flight of stairs, I hear my husband come through the door from work. For some reason, he also starts up the stairs, just a flight behind me. I walk past my son's room into the library.

I hear my husband knock on his door. "Brieson?"

At the exact moment my husband is opening the door, I am ten feet away sliding that book into place, floating on a crowd of ethereal approval.

Then my husband's tone sharpens. "Brieson!"

Day 0: Call 911

I WILL NOT SHARE ALL THE DETAILS OF THAT NIGHT WITH YOU—JUST a few that were surprising in retrospect.

It was apparent from the first moment I ran into the room that Brieson was gone. Even though I had never encountered a recently dead body before, I knew instinctively that nothing could be done.

After the initial moments of shock, my husband said, "I guess we call 911?"

Immediately, with a surety that arose from no prior experience or thought—and yet it was as if I had scripted this moment from countless rehearsals—I say, "No! No . . . let's spend a moment with him. Alone."

Looking back, I can only say that this was revelatory reflex. At this point in my life, I was uneducated in what happens after an emergency call is dispatched, but God knew. He knew all that would transpire in the next several hours and days, and most importantly, He knows me.

He knows how emotionally reticent I am—how slowly I process feelings. He knows that I think first, *then* I decide how I will feel without interference from others. He prompted me to stop and take this moment because it turned out that we would never be completely alone with Brieson's body again. Even though we were promised it several times during the examination and funeral proceedings, it never actually happened. In each of those future instances, something intervened to prevent it.

I suppose this may seem like extraordinarily odd behavior (as the grief counselor I later visited made abundantly clear). I assume most suicides are moments of pure panic, confusion, terror, and chaos. I can't explain it to you—I can only say that after the first few moments (not even a full minute), it was not any of those things. A kind of reverence settled over the room. I felt piercing desolation but also mental clarity and a tender control, as if I had foreseen this, prepared for it, and was precisely following prescribed best practices instead of the abrupt plunge off an unseen cliff that it actually was.

Because of my meticulous study of near-death experiences, the plan of salvation, and angels, I was gently reminded that a person's spirit is often in the room when their body is discovered. I felt confident that Brieson was trying to speak with us in this moment—doubtless apologizing and just beginning to realize the depth of his act. He was probably trying to tell us something, frustrated with his lack of ability to communicate with us.

So I sat on his bed, beside his very still body, and thought as hard as I could, "I know, Brieson. I know. It's okay. We love you." I received no communication from him. I waited . . . but nothing. There was a pervading peace, love, and calmness, but no sense of Brieson in the room.

My focus was not on myself or my feelings but turned outward, immediately outward to him, without condemnation. Even as I write this, I recognize how implausible it sounds. I expect your vision of how things like this occur is probably colored by television dramas and sensational novels, as mine once was. That's why I wanted to share it with you. From the very beginning, God was stepping me through this, and it was not like anything I would have previously supposed or conceived.

Day 0: Prime Numbers

WITHIN THE FIRST TWO OR THREE MINUTES OF DISCOVERING Brieson, my objective becomes finding some sort of confirmation. My mind is flipping through possibilities, mining data, opening tabs, starting search engines. Then one thought fills the screen: today is March 23, 2017. Three. Twenty-three. Two thousand and seventeen. All prime numbers.

A small gear slides into place and locks down.

This is something Brieson and I share: a love of prime numbers, especially dates composed of prime numbers. There has always been something inside me that feels the click of resolution when digits are prime numbers, as if I have reached the most basic understanding. I have the final answer—nothing else to derive or factor.

That *something* now acknowledges that yes, indeed, it *is* time. This is the time, although there have been no previous suicide attempts, no threats, and no suggestions.

I can feel a curtain being drawn across the stage. Even though it should be the middle of the first act, I know the play is over. I have a sense of standing in the theater staring at the still-swaying curtain, hoping the play will resume, while those around me are already getting up and gathering their things. I can hear the scuffling backstage, but the part for my viewing is complete.

Those three prime numbers—3, 23, 2017—resolve me. There is some complex equation behind all of this, but someone else has done the computations, solved for the unknown *x,* and is handing me the answers: 3, 23, 2017. These are the factors; the calculations will be explained later. I am assured that all the communicative, associative, and distributive laws have been followed. Both sides equal out in the end.

I am thinking, *Open the curtain! There is more to be done. This story isn't finished.* Yet all the while I feel the sense of two lines being drawn below the answer and the pencil being laid down.

Day 0: Coroner's Expectations

AT THIS POINT IN MY LIFE, I HAD NO EXPERIENCE WITH EMERGENCY response procedures. I did not know the commotion that would ensue once that 911 call was placed. After those three numbers are dialed, it all becomes surreal.

How is this happening to us? We have emergency tape in our front yard. A fire truck with flashing lights is in our driveway. Who have we become?

A suicide requires an investigation and hours and hours of scrutiny. We are questioned by multiple emergency response teams: firefighters, police officers, detectives, and the coroner. We fill out paperwork. We wait as they go through everything in his room: his computer, his books, his clothes, his phone. We wait and wait and wait as they briskly walk back and forth. We are not allowed in his room. We wait in the family room.

Over six hours later, I hear someone talking to me. I look up and search for the body connected to this voice. It's another man with gloves. He is telling me that they are bringing Brieson's body down the stairs on a stretcher. It is now well past midnight. Over the last hour, we have been told by numerous personnel that this moment is coming. They want us to be prepared to see our son again.

Four men jockey the stretcher down the stairs and into the front room. They are just sets of gloves to me—I have never looked at their faces. Now they wait for us to have one last look at him. They seem firm that we must do this. There is an expectation here. We must see him one last time before he leaves this house forever. It is customary. They step back a respectful distance.

I step up to the stretcher—to Brieson, even though this is not Brieson anymore. This feels plastic in every way, artificial and contrived. Then, quite suddenly, I sense his presence. I realize he has been here the entire time and now is merely walking up behind me to see his body for himself.

He is not going to leave in the hearse with them. He is right here, right next to me, standing beside me looking down at his own body. I feel as if I could cut my eyes to the right and meet his worried expression—not worry for himself but for me. Brieson is here to see me through this moment and assure me that this is a formality, not a finality.

I whisper, as convention apparently dictates, "Goodbye, Brieson." It seems odd to bid farewell to someone who is both next to me and simultaneously rolling away from me.

As I watch them lift the stretcher out the door, I feel no heightened loss because that body has gone. Brieson—the real Brieson—is standing by me watching it go.

Day 1a: The Gift of Quick Response

I AWAKE THE NEXT MORNING TO A BRIEF PAUSE OF OBLIVION, THEN IT all floods back, even sharper because it is a new puncture on a fresh wound. I roll over, heavy with this new weight.

Our first task is for my husband and I to call our brothers and sisters to tell them. (We called each of our children the previous night before we called 911.) All our brothers and sisters live in other states many hours away, and none will come until the funeral.

We then look at each other and take in a breath of courage because the next call will be the one that spreads the news to locals. We know that just one call will be all that is needed—the word will be out. We lie in bed staring at the ceiling for a few minutes. Then I look at my husband. "Okay," I say. "Let's do it."

We actually only send three texts. Then I get up and begin the day. I shower and dress. It's about 8 a.m. now. My husband is in the shower, and I hear the doorbell ring.

As strange as this sounds, I go to the door without a thought in my head that this will be about Brieson. It has only been twenty minutes since the first text. My hair is still wet. But when I open the door, there stands Kathy, a woman from our ward. She's holding a fistful of flowers, her eyes wide, her face concerted.

I am completely stunned—speechless for a moment. She must assume this is from grief, but it's really from astonishment. I had absolutely no expectation of this. None at all. Kathy is not someone I know well.

She must have instantly dropped what she was doing, picked up flowers from somewhere, and driven straight to our house the microsecond she received word this had happened. No hesitation, no second-guessing herself—just pure desire to help, as if she had come purposefully to pull our still-gasping faith from the rubble. She seems to instinctively realize that to save a person from a burning building means risking your own self as well. There is some peril in this visit, and I can tell that she fully recognizes the risk of it and is prepared to see it through.

Only now do I realize how devastating it would have been if we had sent out texts and no one had come. Kathy's gift of immediacy stopped me from ruminating. This seemed very close to what seeing an angel must be like: my thoughts were interrupted, my mind diverted, and I stood in awe and wonder, immediately thrumming with something gentle.

I invite her in, unsure what to do, how to receive her, or what to say. We stumble through a conversation. I don't remember a single word of it. Her compassion is felt by every part of me, but I cannot react to it. I am halfway between icy and thawing—that point where you feel frozen and yet in pain all the same.

Day 16: The Gift of Converging

MY HAIR NEVER GETS ATTENDED TO BECAUSE THE VISITORS FROM church never stop coming. Perhaps they understand what Elder David A. Bednar once taught: "There are principles related to receiving revelation. For example, President Packer said, 'President Harold B. Lee told me once that inspiration comes easier when you can set foot on the site related to the need for it. . . . President Lee was right!' There is value in being in the place, pondering, praying, and seeking for help."[1]

After Kathy, my friend Charlotte arrives.

Charlotte's visit is especially poignant because she knows about many other things I have been struggling with over the last few years, not just about Brieson. She says very little. We sit across from each other while I hold her tray of meat and cheese. I can see she is so sorry that life is kicking me down so hard at the moment, especially on top of the other struggles. She can see it's piling up. I can tell she's worried whether I might break from all of this, and although I want to reassure her, I can't.

Charlotte is followed by Dana and Marcus, friends from church. I don't remember anything that was said that day. But I will never forget the people who came—the people who arrived without any consideration of how we might receive them. They only wanted to assure us that we were loved and supported.

Some on the list I knew would come—others are surprising. But every person is a walking message from God, as if God called for angelic envoys and they streamed in with hands held high. They are oblivious to the light they bring; they literally glow. I can hardly take it in. They are pulsing with energy and love. It is so thick I can almost reach out my hand and touch the essence of it—a soft, pliable field that I don't need to change at all to fit into because it easily conforms around me.

They come to look in on me, but it is me who cannot stop looking at them. I can tell that they are unaware of Who they represent. They shuffle in as if they are just ordinary people, but somewhere between their house and mine, they have been clothed in some sort of glory, and I can feel it like a living presence. How do they carry it so casually?

---

1. David A. Bednar, "An Evening with Elder David A. Bednar," Feb. 7, 2020, https://www.churchofjesuschrist.org/study/broadcasts/an-evening-with-the-general-authorities/2020/02/bednar-highlights.

Day 1c: List Making

I MAKE LISTS EVERY DAY—MULTIPLE LISTS SOMETIMES. IT SEEMS LIKE the most logical thing in the world to do right now. After the first person comes, I go into my room, open my notebook, and write the following:

Day 1. 8:00 a.m. Kathy Ganem—flowers

This was an intentional act—the recording of events. I never considered the purpose behind it. Perhaps unconsciously this was a way to get things in order. Lists are how I have always organized my day and my life. It is a way to confront turmoil, and at this moment, turmoil was swirling all around me. Putting ink to paper seemed like a natural response.

This list helped me to capture the moments, even define them. I made little notes by the names: "book," "unashamed," "cactus," "fear," just short words that came to me. Now some of the words have no context for me, but that record is precious to me—a portfolio of spiritual deposits.

First, and most obviously, this list became a reminder of who came. That entire first week is foggy and muddled in my mind. Some things are completely forgotten, buried beneath a deluge of thoughts and feelings. I was conversing and listening with every person who came, but after they left, I sometimes felt as if we had merely passed on the street with barely a nod.

Second, this list became a graphical representation of the accumulation of love that was being offered to me—a concrete record of indefinable offerings. That list currently contains over 573 distinct names. (And I missed some—I'm sure I did.) It is visual evidence of the magnitude of love that was shown to me. Just seeing that list—not even reading the individual names, just seeing the length of the list—makes my heart swell. When I zoom in and examine the individual cogs that make up this complex machinery of support, I begin to appreciate the orchestration of God.

Third, this list was a directory for the letters of gratitude I would write later. If I had had to think back and remember who came and who did what, I would have given up. That kind of exacting mental effort was overwhelming to consider in the heavy days following, which was exactly when I needed this list the most. But since I had already made the list, it was easier to pick up a pen and start writing. In terms of resiliency and healing, writing the letters of gratitude was possibly the most important thing I did for my own self-care.

Fourth, this list was a shield against self-pity. I had never taken the time to consider how many ways there are to show love. Most of the things done for me I had never previously recognized as indications of caring. This book comes from that list. It is easy to believe during those long days (that fold into weeks that stretch into months) that no one has been more ignored than you have been. But with my list, I could quickly see at a glance that no one has ever been as loved as I have been.

Fifth, this was a collection of precious impressions. Elder Richard G. Scott once said, "You will find that as you write down precious impressions, often more will come."[2] Now, I would never have thought that a list of names would be a "precious impression," but it is. I have found that reviewing and following up are powerful means for receiving confirmation or new revelation from the Holy Ghost. This list has become a kind of excavation site for inspiration—the deeper I dig into it, the more I return to it, and the more I discover God in every single name and every single act.

This book is evidence of the growing revelation from this list. As I consider each act, more understanding and more discernment comes concerning the gifts that were offered. I see them more clearly now, three years later, than I ever did then.

---

2. Scott, Richard G., "To Acquire Knowledge and the Strength to Use it Wisely" (Brigham Young University devotional, Jan. 23, 2001), 1, speeches. byu.edu.

Day 1d: The Gift of In-Person Support

At first, I waited for arriving visitors to broach the subject, to offer some words of wisdom, to ask the questions, to start the conversation. I thought they must have come because they had advice or understanding to give. They must have come with something to say to me. People don't just come over for no reason, right?

So I waited. Sometimes we sat in silence for several minutes. I was waiting for them to say what they had come to say. I was still puzzling over why people were coming. Slowly it became apparent to me that no one knew what to say or do—not them, not me. There are no words for this—none at all. Instead, these people were coming just to offer themselves, to concretely evidence that they were concerned about us and loved us. It wasn't just well wishes or kind thoughts but whole bodies coming as living witness.

This may be one of the things that makes grief so awkward; both parties are waiting for the other one to step up and assume some kind of ownership in easing the moment or showing the way. In the first few visits, the silences seemed to stretch on and on until it felt as if something needed to give. It took me some time, but eventually I realized that something was me.

No one teaches you how to do this. This is a true "in the trenches" kind of act. People came without any knowledge of our emotional, spiritual, or physical state. They just came. When this finally registered with me, I made a decision: I am going to receive this generous and courageous gift. They came with one object only: to be of service to us, even though they were completely unsure of what that service might be.

The visits became much easier after I opened myself up to these offerings. I tried not to turn away when it didn't come in the way I wanted it to come or it wasn't said the way I wanted it to be said. I just accepted their contributions like I would any other gift and thanked them for it.[3]

I knew I could only receive these gifts if I answered the knocks. So I opened and invited them in.

They came warily, just like you would imagine someone stepping into a crime scene—because that's exactly what it was, I realized with a shock. Most people want to drive by a crime scene, look at it, and get back to their schedules, but these people wade right in.

The sheer daring of this I appreciate from the depths of my heart. It is a magnificent tribute. As days go by, a small idea begins to form in my mind. Everyone comes to give me something: acceptance and support. Their very presence sends me the most important message I will ever receive: you are not alone.

I remember something a desert survival trainer once told me. All the people trained in solo survival are perfectly capable of enduring forty-eight hours in the wilderness. Even people who are untrained are capable of that. The test is not in technique or knowledge; instead, it is a test of self-confidence. There is something about human companionship that eases the mind and sharpens the courage. Alone, our doubts increase and we often cave in. These friends were not going to allow this to happen to me. Their presence eased my doubts and lifted my resolve.

Some bring flowers and some bring food, but some come empty-handed and voiceless and stunned. I appreciate every flower, casserole, and paper plate because they are concrete representations of the real gift they bring: their presence. I am determined to receive and honor it by opening every knock, answering every text, and engaging in every visit. They have come to soothe my pain, and in some divine transaction, some part of it leaves the house with them.

---

3. For more understanding about this, see Lisa Clark Valentine, "'Yes, and . . .': The Creative Art of Living" (Brigham Young University devotional, July 20, 2021), speeches.byu.edu. As author Toba Beta once said, "It's so tempting to resist a little gift when you're expecting the otherwise" ("Inspiring Quotes about Gifts and Giving," accessed Aug. 16, 2023, https://www.ugandaempya.com/quotes-about-gifts/). I had to learn to appreciate the spirit with which things were offered. Everyone came with a desire to help me.

Alma tells us that Jesus "shall go forth, suffering pains and afflictions . . . of every kind . . . [and] take upon him the pains and the sicknesses of his people" (Alma 7:11). Is this what these people are doing? Going forth to take some of my pain? That is how it seems to work.

With each departure, a small edge of the pain is smoothed. The burden isn't just the loss of Brieson, which they can never retrieve; this loss also includes a loss of many other things as well. And somehow, their coming tells me that they see me as I have always been. I have not been diminished in their eyes. Instead, they come to assure me that they love me just the same. That offering restores my belief that I have all the tools and support I need to meet this difficulty.

Day 1e: The Gift of Experience

MANY PEOPLE BRING FLOWERS, SOUPS, BREADS, DESSERTS, PLATES, cups, napkins, and water bottles on this first day. All are appreciated. But there is only one gift I still have from that first day: Pam's gift.

Of course, Pam is the visitor I most want to see—the person who knows, *really* knows, what we have just gone through in the last eighteen hours. She arrives later in the afternoon, casually and without advice. She hands me an article and tells me to read it later. I immediately forget it and set it on the countertop, not to be discovered again for weeks but then a needed gem.

She also gives me a cactus. It turns out she will not be the only person to bring me a cactus—you will learn of the other later. It was a "coincidence" that I think is not a coincidence at all.

This cactus is a singular and symbolic gift—one that only Pam can offer. She is giving me a visual representation of grief, an experience that often defies the power of words. The symbolism is not lost on me. Cacti are unapologetic, hardy succulents that adapt well to extreme aridity and are still able to survive. They not only survive but actually thrive in apparently scorched and barren earth. Cacti often appear injurious and forbidding, something to avoid, yet within their spongy flesh flows gallons of living water.

I set Pam's cactus on my window ledge, and it has been there ever since. Sometimes I have forgotten to water it for weeks (maybe months), but there it still patiently waits. It requires little of my time or attention because its inner resources keep it from wilting. A cactus doesn't compete with the roses of life; it blooms under harsher conditions—quite often, in fact.

There is something about seeing this cactus there on the windowsill that momentarily satisfies an unnamed thirst in my heart. When I take a moment to notice it, without fail I think of Pam. And when I think of Pam, I remember what she said after Ryan died: "We will not be ashamed."

Day 2a: The Gift of Encouragement

MY OLDEST DAUGHTER, CARISSA, GOES OUTSIDE TO GET SOMETHING from her car this morning and finds dozens of paper hearts and notes stuck all over our yard: a special heart for every child and every grandchild, all with short sentiments of love.

Carissa comes back into the house and calls to me and her two daughters, Saige and Aspen. She takes us back outside where we carefully step between the hearts, picking them up and reading through them. All of these are from my Jane Austen–loving friends, some who live many miles away from me.

"Heart attacking" is a well-known service in our church, one I have done myself, but I have never had anyone do it for me. As I stand on the sidewalk and watch Saige and Aspen excitedly picking up the hearts and asking their mom to read them, I get this absolute certain feeling of just knowing. It seems I am at the bottom of a dark well, but someone is coming. Someone has a rope ladder or a pulley or something, and they are on their way to get me.

Day 26: The Gift of Open Doors

TODAY OUR FRONT DOORKNOB FINALLY BROKE, COMING RIGHT OFF IN my hand. It has been wobbling for months, but today it just completely stops latching and falls off. Before my husband can go to the hardware store and get another one, people start coming.

Each person is passing through that door twice, coming and going. Almost everyone comments on the gaping hole in the door where the lock and tumbler should be. Ironically, this conversation usually takes place on the way out: "Oh, I see you lost your doorknob." We nod or shrug. Then the visitor says, "If there is anything—*anything*—we can do, let us know." Then they carefully ease the door shut with their fingers through the cross bore, pulling it against the frame. The door often bounces back open a few inches and they try again.

We aren't offended by this—not at all. We find it humorous actually. We realize that everyone is perhaps looking for something more substantial to contribute, more oriented to repairing our poor souls than our door holes.

This broken knob became symbolic to me in retrospect. I am incredibly private with my feelings and really my life in general. But this door, which could not be locked or latched, invited everyone in and sent a clear message to keep no one out.

"Let them in," God seemed to say. "All of them. Any time of day or night, just open up and let them in. They bring what you need."

In the beginning I always answered the door. I had never considered having someone else do this for me. Later I realized the benefit this brought. Opening my own door did not allow me to avoid anyone. I had to face the compassion, the questions, the blunders of every visitor. After a little bit, it does get tiring, but it also builds a certain kind of resiliency and openness.

With each visitor, the same things are said, the same story gone over, and that is a type of rehabilitation as I reframe and rephrase and revisit the same questions again and again. This repetition becomes a path to understanding and acceptance. Each retelling and each visit is slightly, ever so slightly, different.

I can't recall a single conversation that I would describe as revelatory, but their collective power was undeniable. I didn't understand it then, and I don't understand it now, but in the midst of the reciting, everything became filled with meaning, and I saw God both implied and explicit in every detail.

God reaches out to me every moment of the day. But I usually shut the door, turn the lock, and wait inside for a definable knock. But now I am so full of holes that I am practically threadbare. I have no ability to block or shield anything, and because of that, I feel God's love so easily. He doesn't need to knock—He just walks right in.

Day 3a: The Gift of Strength

JUST LIKE EVERY SUNDAY, I WALK INTO CHURCH. IT IS EXACTLY THE way it has always been. Not a particle has changed—same benches, same walls, same people. But I see it all very differently now. Nothing in this world seems ordinary anymore.

I think back to last Sunday. Last Sunday, I stood in the parking lot and talked to Bart, a man from the ward, about Brieson. He asked about him. Because so few people ever do that, this memory is now heightened to me. I see the telltale fingerprints of God's hand at work. Seven days ago. Seven. I was completely oblivious to God's impressions in my life then, but they seem so apparent now. His fingerprints are smeared everywhere in this tragedy—not as a culprit but as a probing, healing agent.

I feel the studied nonchalance of everyone in the room—everyone pretending that nothing has changed, tactfully trying to step around the landmines by feigning unawareness of our presence in the room. Eyes skitter away, and steps are slightly accelerated as they walk by. I feel nothing about this—nothing at all. The depth of sadness does not allow greater pain. Maybe they are pinpricks, but they don't register against the stabbing I have experienced.

Judd walks over to our row. My husband stands up to greet him and bursts into tears. They hug. This draws almost everyone's attention. I see the boldness of what Judd has done. Probably the very thing he most wanted to avoid has happened: a grown man cried in public. But Judd stands his ground, ready to absorb whatever emotion he can. It's a true act of strength.

I feel no anger toward anyone who avoids us. How can I? I did exactly the same thing to Pam. It's human nature. But in a strange twist, I now realize that this feigned ignorance takes more energy than acknowledgment would. I can see how uncomfortable they are. We don't receive much instruction in how to approach a grieving person. They probably wonder why we are even here. We have certainly made things awkward for everyone.

This makes it easy for me to fall into the idea that no one knows what I am feeling. This situation may be a little more than I can assimilate. But just as I start into this self-conversation, I see Pam walk by and realize that my situation is more universal than I might want to admit. Everyone carries secret heartache. Some sorrows are more public, well-known, and culturally acceptable, but all of us harbor something that seems it will isolate us from humankind forever.

So I stay, internally squirming, reminding myself that all people suffer. Even Jesus Christ suffered, and Alma tells us that He did this so He could know how to succor His people (see Alma 7:12). Now I cannot leave. It seems a betrayal of the highest kind to walk out of His house—the One who atoned for this very moment for me.

I sit quietly, but I am far from feeling reverential or worshipful. I practically sprint from the building when the service is over.

Day 36: The Gift of Courage

I HEAR A KNOCK ON THE DOOR. I'VE BEEN EXPECTING IT. MY FRIEND Ashley texted to say she is coming—a kind of tribute to my old nature. She knows I don't like people dropping by, or at least I didn't before this happened. Now it doesn't bother me. What could possibly be worse than this? What can I possibly have to hide when I've already been gutted?

I open the door. Ashley stands about a step back from the doormat, almost like a stray dog. She exhibits watchful caution, her posture one of almost instant flight, wanting to be accepted and fearing to be kicked. Ashley is one of my very close friends and has stood on that porch dozens of times before, but now it feels like unfamiliar territory.

I see this same posture frequently on the other side of the door. I have almost come to expect it: the fear, the hesitation. Yet all of it overridden by the deeper desire to help—a true testament of courage

Later I would read this quote from Brené Brown: "One of the most valuable gifts in my life was from my mom. She taught us to never look away from pain. The lesson was simple and clear: Don't look away. Don't look down. Don't pretend not to see hurt. Look people in the eye. Even when their pain is overwhelming. And when you're hurting and in pain, find the people who can look you in the eye. We need to know we're not alone—especially when we're hurting."[4]

Ashley exemplifies that lesson to perfection. I am grateful to all who came, but the ones I admire the most are those who came completely alone. They came during the raw, resonating, and trembling time and stepped boldly into it. With some kind of inner fortitude, they dared to risk the unknown. They could have met with anything behind that door—they didn't know. But their compassion superseded their apprehension. I guess you can't test courage cautiously, and like Ashley, they rode in with their colors flying.

A few minutes later Kevin arrives, alone as well, again with the same caution at the door. I invite him in, and we all end up talking and laughing about lining up Ashley with Kevin's friend. Everything is easy and familiar: two people I have always respected for their analytical minds, coming by to just share stories and ideas. We do not speak of funerals or grief. Nothing melancholy enters the conversation, and no words of wisdom are exchanged.

When they leave and I close the door behind them, somehow I know that because I renewed my baptismal covenants today, God fulfilled His part. He sent two people who are conscientious covenant-keepers to "mourn with those that mourn . . . and comfort those that stand in need of comfort" (Mosiah 18:9).

---

4. Brené Brown, *Atlas of the Heart: Mapping Meaningful Connection and the Language of Human Experience* (New York: Random House, 2021), 271–272.

I recognize that I have stumbled today, but God did not berate me or lecture me. Instead, He sent those who do His work in His way: by gentleness, meekness, and love unfeigned. As I turn from the door, the touchy, raw thing that has been floating around inside of me since sacrament meeting settles like sand on the ocean floor.

Day 3c: The Gift of Loyalty

EVERYONE APPRECIATES, ADMIRES, AND APPLAUDS SUCCESS. ANYONE who is famous must have experienced this. The more well-known you are, the more people want to claim an acquaintance with you. *She's my mom's neighbor. I went to third grade with her. I met her in a restaurant in Palm Beach.* We all want to be associated with success.

But someone who will come when you are at your lowest, worst, and least is the definition of a friend. Such a person acts as a stabilizer in the upheaval. I have many such friends, I am coming to realize. But there's one in particular who stands out—someone who has known me since I was thirteen years old. Without hesitation, without a moment's consideration, I texted, "Kellee, Brieson killed himself last night. Will you come?"

I never thought about it again. I knew, with perfect surety, that she would come. Regardless of difficulty or inconvenience, she would come. She would not reject me; she has never rejected me, though innumerable opportunities have presented themselves. In fact, through the past forty-four years, she has always been there for every major occasion of my life.

I think the best people—the people I am most drawn to—possess a knack for seeing positive intentions in all interactions, have a desire to help others at whatever the cost to themselves, and demonstrate a tenacious dependability in times of crisis. Kellee is the best of the best.

I have learned that compassion has a difficult time coexisting with judgment. I think this is because judgment requires a distancing. That distance is needed to compare, to contrast, to set side-by-side, measuring one against another. That means we have to step back and step away.

Compassion does the opposite: it zooms in. Closeness facilitates accepting, immersing, and appreciating the innate beauty without reference to anything else. In this situation, I need someone who can zoom in pixel-tight, and there is no one who can provide that like Kellee.

I am completely myself with Kellee. She knows the junior-high self, the awkward high-schooler, the newlywed, the unsure mother, the frustrated teenager mother, the mother-in-law, the empty-nester, the grandmother, the teacher, the tennis player, and dozens of other versions of me. She has seen all these identities up close and personal. While most people only see a few sides of me, she has the entire panorama.

She will help me enlarge and develop this next self, shortening the exposure time, keeping the main things in focus, smoothing the background, and reframing until it all fits.

Because of this long-standing panoramic view of my life, there's no one I trust more at my back. Grief often feels like solitary battling. Right now, it is purely defensive and fraught with the anxiety of always checking over my shoulder or giving half-attention to what might be circling behind me. But just one person who knows my background allows me to focus on the task ahead—what lies right in front of me. Kellee's presence gives me the confidence to look forward, knowing she will take care of all kinds of things behind me.

And she does. So many things, in fact, that I only learn about some of them months and even years later.

Day 4a: The Gift of Understanding

I DON'T KNOW THE ALGORITHM FACEBOOK USES, BUT OVER THE NEXT few days, I see numerous articles in my feed about suicide. One pops up this morning, very early. I'm lying in bed scrolling along, and I click on one. I later find out that it was written by a man who took his own life not long after publishing it.[5] The article is about what it feels like to be contemplating suicide.

He compares it to being on the top floor of a high-rise building. You are standing out on the window ledge because there is a fire in your room. No one can see the fire but you. There seems to be no way to get down out of the building without passing through the raging fire. You believe that your own actions have taken you to this floor, and now all that remains are two choices: burn or jump.

You decide to jump because it seems like the less painful of the alternatives. As you teeter on the ledge, looking down and ready to jump, you see all of your family and friends below on the pavement. They're yelling, "Don't jump! We love you! Don't jump! We're coming for you!"

But they can't feel the heat of the fire. They can't see the flames growing closer. They don't know what you are experiencing—the desperation and the urgency.

You do not doubt that your loved ones want to help you. You know that they love you. But they are so far away, and you feel certain they will never reach you in time. In fact, you fear they may get burned themselves if they get too close.

For you, with the fire leaping and scorching and in this moment of desperation, there just doesn't seem to be any way to be saved. Their efforts will be futile. You are anxious and stressed and looking for an escape, but you can't find it and time is running out. You want to live as much as the next person, but your options seem so limited. All that appears left to your control is the way in which you will die. So you choose the avenue that seems like the quickest end to the pain.

If it is possible to feel a paradigm shift, then this was like an earthquake in terms of unsettling me and shaking my thoughts around. This seemed like more than just a random essay—it felt like a pointed message for me. Quite suddenly, I saw suicide as the monstrosity that it is—not in my individual tragedy only but as the beast that has always stalked the earth. This malady is not new; it is a long-held

---

5. See David Foster Wallace, *Infinite Jest* (New York: Back Bay Books, 2006), 696.

weapon of destruction wielded by devils of prey, the modern-day tale of the monster in the forest. We all know it is there, but we hope that by ignoring it, whispering its name, it won't find us.

We are usually unconscious of the many forces at play around us—gravity, the second law of thermodynamics, gratitude, thermal heat, guardian angels. When I list them like that, it doesn't seem very scientific, but it is. All of these forces have power. These invisible forces make concrete differences in our lives, but we are mostly oblivious to everything except what we can see with our very limited vision. I am suddenly horrified by my own naivety.

The next logical step is for me to consider how I might have stopped this beast or at least caged him. *Could I have made more of a difference? Could I . . .* But my train of thought is stopped—utterly halted in mid-air, as it were. A sweet feeling, thick with purity and calmness, settles over me. My mind pushes back against it, but it remains firmly blocking this avenue of thought.

Then a knowledge is placed inside of me—not through my mind, but as if it has always been a part of me and merely rising to the surface. *You acted on what you knew. You said what you could. You were the person you needed to be. Brieson knows this, and that you love him.*

There is a pause—a heavy one. As I let these ideas pass through my heart and reach my mind, I begin to slowly dismantle them and fit them to real-life experiences. I sense an unhurried waiting as I do this, like a teacher patiently standing beside me as I work an equation. After a few moments I mentally and emotionally (but tentatively) assent to these thoughts. My heart is lurching along behind them but finally settling into a new cadence.

Then, in a rush, this phrase comes into my mind as if thrown back as the door is closed: *He will come for you and guide you into the other worlds you have not yet imagined.*

Wait! What? But there is only an echoing feeling to the question. The answerer is gone, and I am left to ponder. I am filled—actually *brimming*—with joy and anticipation. Those are two feelings I don't think I should be experiencing during grief, and yet there they are—in super abundance.

I exit Facebook, turn over in bed, and set down my phone, wide awake though it's far from morning. I consider what this means. We could never understand why Brieson made the choices he did. He had many people who were reaching out to him. Often the prevailing idea with suicide is that they are all alone in their lives, and if only they had someone to talk to, they wouldn't do it.

But haven't we all felt the inner restless spirit that craves connection, even while surrounded by family and friends? Sometimes I have felt as if everyone around me is plumbing the shallows while I am desperate for a deep-sea dive, yet this doesn't drive me to thoughts of ending my life. I realize that something is being taught to me, but it is just beyond the edge of my understanding, and I cannot pull it into my awareness.

I have to save this article. I have to remember that whatever I learn in the future, I was doing the best I could in the moment with the information I had. Later I may find something that would have been the key to his survival, but today I am as baffled as I have been for the last several years over what Brieson was experiencing. I don't know what would have saved him. He had family. He had friends. He had plans. He had financial support, emotional support, spiritual support, social support. Something else was at play here. He was governed by something interior; his exterior world seemed to be in place.

We try to protect our world with lights, alarms, firewalls, and locked mechanisms, but somehow this kind of monster gets in anyway. We fear monsters because they seem unbeatable, unpredictable, and uncontrollable. That's why suicide feels so scary and shocking. The monsters you can see are easier to defeat. The monsters that live inside us always seem one step ahead. Perhaps that's what he felt—like he had to destroy the monster inside of him before it got out and damaged more than himself (see 2 Nephi 9:10–11).

Day 46: The Gift of Small and Simple Things

I AM RECEIVING MORE TEXT MESSAGES, PHONE CALLS, AND EMAILS than I can reply to. I try to answer some of them every night. My cousin Wendy calls me from Montana where she is visiting her daughter. We have been cousins all our lives and friends since I was about eight years old.

When we were in elementary school, we would pick dandelions and make them into chains. We would sit on her sidewalk bridge and dip them in ditch water to curl them up. Back then we didn't know they were worthless weeds. I guess that's the best description of Wendy: she notices what others overlook—the simple, ordinary things—and makes them memorable and something to be cherished. She has an innocent appreciation of life and people that never fails to draw everyone in.

Wendy just visited us a month ago. Brieson presented her with a lemon meringue pie he had made as soon as she walked through the door. Wendy reminds me of that moment and how Brieson helped her organize her phone and showed her how to send pictures. She recounts him taking videos of us, challenging us to ride the hoverboard, going to the comedy show with us. She is in shock that he is gone since she was one of the last people to see him alive.

As she is reminiscing about these things, I am reminded of something deeper: People are not valuable because of their looks, their money, or even their achievements. People are valuable because of what they give: love, kindness, generosity, and gratitude. And *how* they give it is what makes them irreplaceable. That's what everyone's story really is—what every funeral is really about: this person's unique expressions of love offered to this world. Some little things can be such crucial things.

Dandelions will always bring Wendy to mind, just like prime numbers will always make me think of Brieson—two strangely small but powerful things they gifted me in this world. They're little things that in isolation seem hardly noteworthy, but in the context of the battles we fight, they become the horseshoe nails:

> For the want of a nail, the shoe was lost.
> For the want of a shoe, the horse was lost.
> For the want of a horse, the rider was lost.
> For the want of a rider, the battle was lost.
> For the want of a battle the kingdom was lost,
> And all for the want of one horseshoe nail.[6]

Dozens of people are offering me horseshoe nails, apologizing because they appear too bent or rusted to be of any use at all. But they are actually the very things that keep me in the battle. Perhaps battles are won more often by these incremental means than we ever imagine.

As Wendy chatters on, I realize that I have not fully appreciated all that she is until this very moment. Her cheerful patience incrementally transforms every person she meets. I imagine that one day we will all stand in heaven applauding the recipients of horseshoe nail awards because only then will we fully see how critical their small contributions were to our lives.

Day 4c: The Gift of Family Support

ALL MY CHILDREN ARE HELPING IN EVERY WAY THEY CAN: CLEANING up Brieson's room, talking to visitors as they arrive, taking care of the kitchen, running errands, looking through phones, and contacting people about the funeral.

Each one is trying to decide what to talk about at the funeral and being supportive and gently caring of me and my feelings. They seem ready to take care of me, but I don't want this. I'm *their* caregiver, not the other way around. Despite their mature response, I can see they are thrown off-balance and wonder if the world will ever right itself again.

I am the focus of everyone's efforts. Even my husband is seen as one degree removed from this tragedy. I wonder at this. Why is the

---

6. Original author unknown.

mother's grief more accepted and expected than the grief of other family members? I had a great deal of life before Brieson, while Kambren and Siearra, his younger siblings, have never lived a single day of their lives without him.

Folding myself away and becoming as much trouble as possible to others, being unable to function, and acting as if I have no hope for the future does not seem like a faith-filled response. I must certainly carry this sorrow, but I do not need to borrow sorrow or escalate it.

I can tell that my children are taking their lead from me. What will I do? What will I say? How will I respond? I need my children to see that my life is going on so that they can feel comfortable going on with theirs. This seems like the responsible response to grief.

I don't want others, especially my children, to feel they must bolster me up. They have grief of their own. Instead, I want them to gain security and hope from me. I realize I am the example they will look to as they try to discern if this gospel teaches truth—whether I believe it with my whole heart, or if it has all just become debris floating in the wind now that the unexpected has occurred.

Several people understand that my family mourns as well. Amanda and Jamie, friends from church, take my youngest daughter, Siearra, to lunch. Jamie and Brianna, my oldest daughter's friends, post videos with Brieson. Carissa, my oldest daughter, has friends in her ward who prepared a travel box of items for their kids for the ten-hour drive to the funeral. My daughter-in-law's friends at work assemble a huge wellness gift basket. Several people come to the funeral just to support my children—people I don't know and who did not know Brieson but who know my other children.

I once heard that art is not meant to be beautiful but is meant to evoke a response of some kind. Does it make you think differently? Feel differently? See differently? Then the piece has done its job. These people who give to my children through creative acts of service evoke an artistic response not only from my children but from me as well.

Day 4d: The Gift of Precedent

This morning Dana, Pam's husband, bursts through the door with two pitchers full of orange juice. He tries to put them in the fridge, but it's stuffed full. After he pushes aside piles of food on the counter and wedges them in, he turns and says, "Just thinking of you and wanted to drop this by." Before we can even get up, he is out the door again.

There are many people who have lost children to suicide. There are many who have lost sons. I am coming to realize that grief is not a rare thing; it is only new to me. This means that I have shoulders to stand on of others who have gone before me, like Dana and Pam.

Their son, Ryan, took his life two years previously. Their graceful and stalwart posture throughout all of it is a beacon of hope for me. I do not have to construct a path through this because they have already put lights along the way. Their example is an indispensable gift.

Sometimes when adversity strikes, we like to think that our situation is so unique that no one could possibly understand what we are experiencing. But like Solomon says, there is hardly anything new under the sun (see Ecclesiastes 1:9). Knowing Pam and Dana gives me immediate concrete models to follow during this challenging time. Pam calls it the gift of second; knowing that you are not the first helps to alleviate some pressure and loneliness. Their mentorship helps us and our ward in ways that are impossible to specify. A great deal of our response is characterized by standing on the shoulders of these spiritual giants.

Death touches us all. There are many people on the broad road of grief. And there are many people who have had deaths by suicide—this is a narrower path, but still it is there. I need not feel alone in this journey. I am just stepping onto it, but it's comforting to realize that there are others continually coming and going along this path, just ahead and just behind me.

The path looks difficult, but it's traversable. Others assure me that it will be life-changing but not life-culminating.

Day 5: The Gift of Uncertainty

WHEN I HAVE HAD PROBLEMS WITH MY CHILDREN IN THE PAST, KIND people have patted me on the shoulder and said, "Don't worry. It will all work out." No one is saying that now.

This is probably one of the most difficult aspects of suicide: there is so much unknown surrounding it. I feel other's apprehension as they struggle to find consoling words when the doctrine isn't clear. There are several videos published by the Church about this situation. Perhaps one of the most helpful things I read came from Ron Rolheiser: "A person dying of suicide dies, as does a victim of physical illness or accident, against his or her will. People die from physical heart attacks, strokes, cancer, AIDS, and accidents. Death by suicide is the same, except that we are dealing with emotional heart attack, an emotional stroke, an emotional AIDS, emotional cancer, and an emotional fatality."[7]

Of course, there is more information on suicide at this point than there has been for decades, but I still do not know much about this topic, medically or doctrinally. But I do believe there is compassion on both sides of the veil when it occurs. I feel that Brieson's future depends on things I will do for him and also upon his acceptance of those things. He has work to do. I have work to do. My influence has not ended. The opportunity is not over. Brieson's future may be uncertain, but it is not hopeless.

President M. Russell Ballard reassured us that "only our Father in Heaven knows the full answer to the questions our hearts ask regarding those who take their own lives. But it is clear that hope exists."[8]

There is a world of difference between hopeless and uncertain. Uncertain is to be unclear or unsure about something. Hopeless is to have no remedy or cure. Apparently, I have to trust the Healer.

---

7. Ronald Rolheiser, *Bruised and Wounded: Struggling to Understand Suicide* (Orleans, MA: Paraclete Press, 2017), 147.

8. M. Russell Ballard, "Suicide: Some Things We Know, and Some We Do Not," *Ensign*, Oct. 1987, 9.

Everything will come at the perfect time. When nothing is certain, anything is still possible.

Day 6: Editing

THIS MORNING, SIEARRA EMAILED ME HER FUNERAL TALK. WE MET as a family a few days ago and talked about the gifts Brieson gave to the world and then narrowed them down, having to leave some out. Then each sibling chose a few topics so that everyone attending the funeral would get a well-rounded idea of who Brieson was without needless repetition. Siearra wanted to talk about Brieson's love for roller coasters.

Now Siearra wants me to check over her talk and see if she is saying everything clearly or if she should change anything. I open the document and start reading through it. In the middle of the talk, she has an analogy about life and roller coasters. I like it. I finish reading through the entire talk and then start to edit a few words here and there.

I leave the roller coaster section just as it is and move to the paragraph below it. Suddenly the computer starts deleting backward each word, letter by letter—not quickly but instead in an almost perfect cadence of one letter per second.

I hit the Escape key and then the space bar, then Delete and Backspace. Nothing stops the progressive deletion. Next, I try Enter, then I get frantic as more and more words disappear. No matter what I try, the words continue to erase from my screen, letter by letter, deliberately. I am jabbing at the keys to no affect. I try Ctrl + Alt + Delete, which has always interrupted anything before, but not this time—the words keep vanishing. I simply sit and watch it happen.

Then, just as suddenly as it began, it stops. The entire section about roller coasters has been deleted to the very period preceding it. Nothing else.

Needless to say, Siearra does not talk about roller coasters at the funeral. Draw your own conclusions, but every member of my family said, without hesitation, "Classic Brieson."

Day 7a: Expanded Stature

WE ARRIVE AT THE FUNERAL HOME TO DRESS BRIESON'S BODY. WE have brought a suit, shirt, belt, and socks—shoes not required. After some initial instruction, the funeral director leads us into an empty chapel. Brieson is on a table at the front of the room. He is covered in a white jumpsuit with a blanket draped over him. My attention is immediately drawn to the blanket since it has a small tear near his knee.

Then my eyes travel upward, taking in the full gurney. Even from a distance, I notice the difference. At first, I think I must be imagining it, but as I get closer, my wonder grows. This makes no sense to me.

Even though he is lying down, there is something about his stature. He seems more mature, older somehow—more like his real age of twenty-four. If you ever met Brieson, you would know he looked like a teenager and was often mistaken for a high schooler. He was a little over six feet tall, but his thinness made him seem much shorter. But now he seems to have filled out and broadened. He is more substantial—more solid. This is so surprising that I can only stare at him.

My heart jolts. *This is how he would have looked if he had not been depressed, carrying those burdens that weighed him down and peeled him away at the same time.*

The funeral director stays in the room with us, guiding us in the best ways to carry out the task of dressing him. The shirt barely stretches across him, and the suit is a tight fit. We even struggle to button the pants that usually hung off him. Finally he is dressed, and we lift him into the coffin. His shoulders seem squeezed into it.

We place his *Lord of the Rings* necklace around his collar and lay it across the tie—he never wore it, but we all felt he would want it with him. The funeral director moves to the back of the room but never leaves.

I stand for a moment looking down at him. This is definitely the Brieson we have always known, and yet it seems we are also meeting a Brieson we are just beginning to know. It was like someone who has been away to foreign lands for a long time and is just coming back to visit—you immediately sense they've changed, though you can't quite say what has altered without more interaction.

A line from Nelson Mandela floats into my mind: "There is nothing like returning to a place that remains unchanged to see all the ways in which you yourself have altered."[9]

This should sound like a remembrance to me, but that's the difference—it doesn't sound like the echo of my own thoughts returning to me but rather like a clarion call from the future, to somewhere or something I have never traversed. I stand by the casket and wonder, *Who is this? Has he changed this much already? It's only been seven days.*

Then drops into my mind an overriding correction: *Seven earth days.* The message is so clear and direct that I almost turn around to see who has said it.

On the way home we are silent, with not even the radio playing. I am staring out the window. *Is that one of the purposes of the story of Creation? If God could make all this in seven days, then what are a few changes in one young son?*

All at once, my image of Brieson blurs. *Is this what people mean when they say they are forgetting what their deceased loved one looks like? Because maybe they don't actually look the way you remember anymore.*[10]

Day 7b: The Gift of Distant Support

ONE OF THE MOST BRACING ACTS OF SUPPORT WAS DONE FOR ME when I wasn't even there.

It's the day before the funeral, and I'm sitting at my computer, going over the program once again. My phone buzzes with a text from

---

9. "There is nothing like returning," BrainyQuote, accessed Aug. 16, 2023, https://www.brainyquote.com/quotes/nelson_mandela_107690.

10. Three years later, I'm preparing a missionary lesson and come across this: "The spirits of our children are immortal before they come to us, and their spirits, after bodily death, are like they were before they came. They are as they would have appeared if they had lived in the flesh, to grow to maturity, or to develop their physical bodies to the full stature of their spirits" (Joseph F. Smith, *Gospel Doctrine*, 5th ed. [1939], 455).

Lynette, a friend I play tennis with. I click on it and an image pops up. I zoom in to get a closer look. It's a photo of some members of my tennis team with their hands clasped together over a racket. Each one wears a bracelet on her wrist. I zoom in further. The bracelets have my son's initials and birth date written on them.

The text reads, "We are thinking of you and dedicating this match to your sweet son, Brieson."

My heart hitches and goes lopsided, allowing something inside of me to break free—like a balloon being caught in a gust and wobbling slowly upward.

I had forgotten that my interclub tennis team had a match this morning. They decided to wear these bracelets in honor of Brieson. Later I find out that Lynette offered a team prayer on the court for me (and if you think that's a normal ritual before a match, it isn't). She passed out the bracelets, then took a picture and sent it to me.

Although it may seem as if it's a tribute to Brieson—who none of them had ever met—it is so much more than that. They are letting me know I have their full support and reminding me, "You are still part of our tribe." I keep looking at it off and on throughout the day, noting the elements that are so much a part of me: tennis, bracelets, prayer.

This is pictorial evidence of the creativity and desire my team is giving to pull me from the sorrow I'm experiencing. I see it clearly. I feel it profoundly. I'm surprised by the immense sense of healing that continues to burst forth like springs of fresh water every time I look at this photo.

I guess this means so much to me because everyone is attentive and kind in my presence, but I wonder what they say when I am not around. What are the conversations then? This act of sympathy is more than some bracelets—it's evidence that they think well of me, even in my absence. They are trying to show me that they still care about me, even behind my back, so to speak.

I eventually put that photo as my phone screen saver, and it remained there for almost three years. I saw it almost daily, and whenever I would pause to look at it, I still got the same floating feeling—an innocent, rising happiness. I have learned that compassion is rarely an accident; it is usually the result of creativity and intention.

Day 9a: The Gift of Camaraderie

I WAKE UP WONDERING WHAT I'M FEELING. THE TRUTH IS THAT I feel almost nothing at all. I've seen enough movies to know what people *expect* me to feel and how I *should* be acting, but that's just it: I don't have the energy to act. I just want to survive this day.

My desires seem at odds: I want to publicly honor Brieson, but I also want to privately grieve.

I have no desire to cry—I just feel empty. When I arrive at the church, I immediately feel the focus is on me. People are coming with the express purpose to see *me*, more so than Brieson.

I don't feel like crying, and I don't feel like smiling either, but I choose to smile because crying takes more energy, at least for me. I smile and smile, and it begins to take on a rictus feel, like something on a skeleton in the corner of the science lab. Yes, like something that everyone has been assigned to study. I am the main specimen, completely uncovered and hung up for inspection.

During the viewing, not many people file through, but those who do express their condolences, hugging and whispering. Although no one is being condescending to me, I am repeatedly struck by pangs of inferiority. The end of this viewing can't come soon enough.

There is a long lull when no one comes, and I continue swimming upstream. Then James and Thresa, friends from church, stride into the room, unhesitant, straight toward me. Thresa grabs me in her customary extended hug and says, quite matter-of-factly, "I can't believe we haven't experienced this yet."

Perhaps that sounds like a strange thing to say, but it is exactly the words to evoke the strongest rush of camaraderie. I can hardly remember anything said to me that day, but this honest, vulnerable moment from Thresa still erases that dark sense of abnormality.

Day 96: The Gift of Explanation

MOST PEOPLE WANT TO BE PART OF THE RESULT, NOT THE PROCESS. But my friend Marolyn is a process person. She engages with me every step of the way. Then when I finally achieve or complete whatever I've been working toward, she celebrates as if I did everything by my own genius and effort. She makes the most minor achievements seem important and worthwhile. Only when I am with her do I realize how many people merely tolerate others. Marolyn, on the other hand, fully invests in everyone around her.

She helps dozens of people—all the time. I have been privileged to be her friend for twenty-eight years, and she has always been helping someone during that time. She never seems worried about extending herself too far. Her concern is focused on what is happening right now, right in front of her. It's those things that she can do something about in real time, and she always finds plenty of work to do.

She is one of the three people I send a text to that first morning. She finally reads the text late in the afternoon and flies into action. She drives straight to our house. When the front door opens, she enters with a whoosh, and the whole room takes on a positive energy, as if we only needed her to plug in the connection.

When considering who would speak at the funeral, she seems like the perfect choice. I know what a difficult task this will be—certainly not anything most people would desire. She hesitates for just a moment and then cheerfully agrees. A day later, she calls me to tell me she wants to give her talk on depression.

My immediate response is, "Uh . . . well, I don't want that to be a topic at the funeral." I'm worried that others will assume too much. It's a strange thing to emphasize.

She begins to explain. I listen, but everything inside of me is against it. I don't want this to be a mental health seminar. Funerals should be spiritually based and heavenly pointing. I don't see how that topic will be comforting or uplifting to anyone, but I leave it up to her.

On the day of the funeral, Marolyn does talk on depression. It's not what I had expected. As I sit there listening to her message, I realize several gifts she is extending: knowledge, transparency, and motive.

People need knowledge, and everyone is looking for the catalyst. Marolyn is helping to tell the story so that each person feels comfortable and perhaps more capable of understanding suicide (and, in turn, understanding us).[11]

Reframing is a valuable tool in the recovery process that requires us to move toward the problem, not away from it. Marolyn has a gift of transparency, and she shares it now because she knows that this kind of unveiling builds trust. We think it's the other way around— that showing only our best side is what makes people like us and bond to us. But after three years, I can assure you that it's the worst moments that have the most Velcro.

With suicide, everyone always wonders, "Why did he do it?" There is a mysterious darkness to this kind of death. Marolyn helps dispel the shadows by shining light directly on the difficult corners, assuring everyone that suicide generally stems from mental illness.

Day 9c: The Gift of Amen

THE SHEER NUMBER OF PEOPLE WHO HELP WITH THE FUNERAL IS incredible. Things are happening that I have no idea are occurring. Seamlessly and softly, things fall into place. Musical numbers are rehearsed, chairs are set up, music is copied, luncheons are planned, tables are set. Every tiny detail is considered and done so carefully.

My friends plan and perform musical numbers, tell me the cheapest place to make copies of the program, set up displays, bake dishes,

---

11. "Another way about thinking of suicide risk and depression is to examine the lives of people who have died by suicide and see what proportion of them were depressed. From that perspective, it is estimated that about 60 percent of people who commit suicide have had a mood disorder (e.g., major depression, bipolar disorder, dysthymia). Younger persons who kill themselves often have a substance abuse disorder, in addition to being depressed" ("Frequently asked questions about suicide," The National Institute of Mental Health, 1999, http://www.nimh.nih.gov/suicideprevention/suicidefaq.cfm).

give talks, set up tables, take pictures, and so much more. I see all this and recognize it, but it all seems removed from me, like watching from behind a camera.

To be honest, I hardly remember who came to the funeral. Thankfully, there is a written record of it and photos to help, although I know many who did not sign the book or were missed in photos.

Later I look through the book, see the names, and am pleasantly gratified by the people who took time to come. Their presence means more to me now than it did then. I guess sometimes we do things in the moment knowing that the reward will be felt in the future. I am feeling those people's efforts now.

Talks are given, songs are sung, tributes are said, testimonies are given, and prayers are offered. Then the entire funeral ends with a unison of "amen." Four little letters, one little word—a common word said thousands of times by me. It is probably the simplest part of the day, but there is nothing simple about the things this word conveys: *amen* means "so be it."

So be it that Brieson has died. So be it that things will never be the same again. So be it that I have no answers to why this was allowed to happen. So be it that the future will keep moving toward me one tick at a time and pass away from me one tick at a time. Amen is to bring our will in accordance with God's will. And every part of this day, from the signatures to the speakers, is meant to help me accept His will. So be it.

Later, as I stand outside the church with people milling about and talking, for the first time I feel something like jagged glass slide down and lodge precariously close to my heart. I feel it right next to my lungs, making it hard for my heart to expand without pain and for my lungs to take a full breath.

I continue to smile despite the awakening knowledge that this glass is now a part of me and will always be there, keeping me from ever being the person I used to be. This jagged glass makes a deep divot in my timeline: I now have my own BC and AD.

Day 9d: The Gift of Continued Support

The funeral is a big landmark, and I just assume that afterward things will kind of go back to normal. People will get back to their lives and the support will dwindle down rather rapidly. That's probably why this gift stuck so strongly in my mind.

I am more tired than I can ever remember being—truly physically sapped after the funeral. The week has been emotional, which was draining all in itself, and then it all culminated in this publicly sensitive event.

I am sitting in the family room with my husband's sister, Sandy, and my best friend, Kellee. My feet hurt and my head aches. The doorbell rings. Expecting it to be one of our family members checking in before they leave to drive back to their respective states, I don't even look up when my daughter Siearra opens the door. I am sitting a dozen feet back and do not recognize the voice.

I get up and walk closer to see that it's Jen, a member of our ward who I hardly know. When I see her standing there, my glass gives a little kick, which I quickly mute—I will check the message later.

She hands Siearra homemade French bread fresh from the oven. I don't remember what she said or what I said, but I will never in a million years forget how that bread tasted or the message that came with it. I have rarely eaten something so delicious—it was as if she had divined my exact palate. I was taken aback by this immediate offering so soon after the funeral. It's as if she was saying, "It's not over for me because I know it's not over for you."

I don't think I have ever had a conversation with Jen. We are passing acquaintances really. I had no expectation whatsoever that she would contact me in any way. The interaction is brief, seconds really. But it caught me up—quick.

As I turn away from the door, my glass unmutes to remind me of the single interaction I had once had with Jen. A few months prior, we were in Relief Society sitting on the same row. There was a seat between us. I wasn't listening to the lesson—I was fully immersed in my own thoughts and feelings. I was trying to figure out what to do with Brieson—trying to overcome the defeated attempts of the past and think in a new way. I felt beaten down and frustrated.

I was jolted out of my reverie when Jen slid past me to give the closing prayer. Immediately after finishing the prayer, she headed back to our row. As I stood up to exit the room, Jen walked right up to me and gave me an earnest hug.

I was shocked. Why would she do that? She might have said something; I don't remember. But it was obvious by her countenance that she saw and felt something and was trying to express it to me without intruding on my privacy. I looked at her for a moment and then just walked out of the room.

As I sliced the French bread, this experience came back to me in full force, and with it these words: "What man is there of you, whom if his son ask bread, will give him a stone? Or if he ask a fish, will give him a serpent? If ye then, being evil, know how to give good gifts unto your children, how much more shall your Father which is in heaven give good things to them that ask him" (Matthew 7:9–11).

This bread was a heavenly reassurance. It was God declaring, through Jen, that despite how it may appear, He had not given me a stone or a serpent. He was intimately aware of my exact tastes and appetites and would be sending me gifts of personalized bread.

Turns out, though, that it wasn't bread after all—it was manna. Because, as you remember, Jesus gave bread only a few times to quell a crisis, but manna came daily, quietly, and dependably—nurturing for over forty years.

Day 9e: The Gift of Friendship

JANICE, A COLLEGE FRIEND OF BRIESON'S WHO I HAD NEVER MET, comes by after the funeral. She says she has something she wants to share with us: the last letter that Brieson wrote to her and a poem he composed.

She reads the letter aloud. Brieson had written to her about catching pigeons in our backyard. He drew an illustration of the trap he built. It was creative, a little manic, and funny—typical Brieson. Then she reads his poem to us:

Keep this poem in your pocket, read it every day
Let it free you of your troubles, drive them out and away
It's not the writing on this paper that will tell you what is true
It is the power of the keeper; that will change what you know
When you feel the fire's piercing mark or the winter's stabbing cold
Remember this poem in your pocket, remember what you hold.

As everyone crowds around her to take a picture, an intonation of loneliness enters my heart and I let it settle deep inside me.

Janice stays for an hour or so and relates many college adventures they had together. Of course, I am unaware of almost all of these times. She is giving us another piece of his life to remember him by. The more she talks, the more I realize the kind of friend she was to him and the encouragement she gave. I had no idea that all of this support and friendship existed for Brieson.

When she gets up to leave, I walk her to the door. She pauses at the threshold and says, "Brieson is my friend." Then her face shuts down as if she has said all that needs to be said, which I guess she has.

Later that night I read the poem over and over while a savoring feeling settles over me. I seem to be in a haze like nothing I have ever experienced before. Everything seems so fragile and so filled with meaning. I see God sending me reassurances piece by piece, line upon line.

Day 10: Looking Up

It's Sunday afternoon and I drive with Kellee to the house in Scottsdale where she is staying. We speak of other things. She is gently aware of my mood—not gushy but respectful. We lay out by the pool and watch Roger Federer win a tennis match on ESPN.

Afterward we get comfortable on the chaise lounge chairs; it is a perfectly mild Phoenix spring day. We begin to talk about Brieson. We wonder things about where he is and what he might be doing.

BAM! A large plop of water hits the ground next to me. The droplet spread is at least three inches in diameter. That's a big drop of water. I look up. Where did it come from? Kellee and I look with surprise first at each other and then heavenward again.

Another large splotch hits the cement. The two patches of water are spaced over two feet apart. More drops begin to fall—not steady streaming but far apart and like a bulbous liquid. I look out into the pool and see the rings expanding from several drops in the pool. Kellee and I look at each other. We look up into the clear blue sky. Not a cloud in sight—absolutely nothing.

It must be a sprinkler system, we reason together, because we are both baffled by where this water is coming from. We walk around the edges of the yard—nothing. We try to peer up over the roof of the house—nothing. We look up into the sky—nothing. There does not seem to be a source for this rain. It is falling out of a cloudless sky.

Then Kellee voices what I've been thinking: "It's Brieson." Our eyes meet in mutual acknowledgment.

The moment seems etched with something that will stay in my memory always—a kind of rising sensation as if the air has become sea-like, shifting around and yet staying in the same place just the same. There is no question in my mind that this is Brieson weeping. Perhaps he's telling me how sorry he is for all the sorrow he has caused—in the past, in the present, and in times yet to come.

"It's okay, Brieson," I telegraph as hard as I can. "It's okay. I love you and I'm not angry with you. I know you carried it for as long as you could."

The space around me seems to open up, and I have that sensation you get when you are on top of a mountain and staring into the open night sky—when you think about the immensity of the universe, the smallness of you, and the wonder of all its beauty and symmetry and precision.[12]

Day 11a: His Room

IT'S TWO DAYS AFTER THE FUNERAL, AND EVERYONE HAS PACKED UP and gone. My husband is back to work for a few hours, the other children back to college, and I am left here alone. Some people are coming over later today, but for now it's just me.

I haven't been in Brieson's room since the night we found him. While I have been talking with visitors and planning the funeral, my children have been cleaning up his room, or at least organizing everything into some semblance of order.

After being home alone for several hours, I climb the stairs. I walk down the hall and take one step into his room. It already feels different. I look around seeing the same bed, the same computer, his boxes, his clothes, his books—all never to be touched or used again.

I thought my jagged glass would be radiating all kinds of messages to me, but instead, it's hard as ice.

I walk over to the desk and punch a key on the computer. The screen opens up—no password needed. My daughter-in-law already checked his cell phone, and again, no password. Brieson always had passwords for everything. Apparently he knew that the emergency personnel would be looking through his things and searching for particular websites, books, and chat rooms. There are websites that provide information on how to prepare for suicide and how to complete it. You can even ask people about their failed attempts.

---

12. Regarding looking up, Elder Carl B. Cook said, "President Monson's encouragement to look up is a metaphor for remembering Christ. As we remember Him and trust in His power, we receive strength through His Atonement. It is the means whereby we can be relieved of our anxieties, our burdens, and our suffering. It is the means whereby we can be forgiven and healed from the pain of our sins. It is the means whereby we can receive the faith and strength to endure all things" ("It Is Better to Look Up," *Ensign* or *Liahona*, Nov. 2011, 34).

But the investigators find nothing on his computer because he has wiped it all clean. To me, this is evidence that he had planned this for a period of time—it wasn't a spur-of-the-moment decision. I check my glass again and feel nothing from it.

I stand in his room for a while. This is still Brieson's room. It has all his things—it's just more cleaned up. The debris is gone, the books are shelved, the bed is made. I wait there, but nothing happens. I try to internally nudge the glass. I want it to give me something, but it remains perfectly silent and cold.

I wonder how long it'll be until it doesn't seem like his room anymore. It still feels as if he could just walk in here at any moment and say, "Mom, what are you looking for?"

Day 116: The Gift of Shared Passions

I can't remember now how it came into my hands—perhaps her mother brought it to me—but Haylee, my friend's 11-year-old daughter, gifts me a miniature stuffed Olaf. He's my favorite Disney character. Haylee and I have always traded Olaf things, but this one is especially endowed with significance.

Haylee remembered this, she searched until she found one, and she bought it for me. No one else in all the world would have thought to give me such a gift. Being atypical imbues it with meaning.

This gift touched me in a way that nothing else has. Haylee is only twelve years old. She's much too young to be worrying about my emotional state, and yet she does—wholeheartedly.

I set Olaf next to my laptop, and I see him several times a day. Without fail, it brings Haylee to mind.

In case you haven't seen it, *Frozen* is an entire movie about rescue. A young girl, Anna, is trying to save her sister, and during the course of her adventures, she gets in a situation where she needs saving herself. That is when Olaf lights a fire for Anna, putting himself at risk in order to save her. I see Haylee the same way: someone taking a risk in order to save me.

Most of us believe we have few gifts, but in reality, we all can give love, compassion, kindness, generosity, peace, loyalty, tact, and many other things. These gifts are really just moments of little rescues, when burdens are lifted and healing is offered.

The offering of these gifts requires a risk, but I can tell you now that playing it safe never saved anyone.

Day 12a: The Gift of God's Presence

MANY PEOPLE SAY TO ME, "I HOPE YOU FEEL GOD WITH YOU."

I can hardly keep from smiling when they say it. Without a doubt this is the case. I feel Him with me at all times—completely blanketed and cushioned.

The reason I smile is due to the paradox of the statement. What people don't seem to understand is that I feel God's attention most powerfully in *their* presence. Their presence makes God seem more tangible because they are physically doing all the things the Holy Ghost does spiritually. When they come to see me, they bring both concrete and intangible assurances from God.

Let me explain. The Holy Spirit performs these kinds of services: brings all things to our remembrance; conveys God's love, attention, and concern; is a companion in a difficult moment; changes the way I feel, think, and act; enlightens me; lifts me; inspires me; and comforts me. All these things are gifts of the Holy Spirit, and when another person—a physical being—does these same things for me, God's presence is magnified.

Therefore, to stand in front of me and say "I hope you feel God with you" is like saying "Shelly, I hope you see me standing here in front of you, talking to you and touching you."

"Yes!" I want to reply. "You are right here—I can see you as plain as day. Oh! And I see you brought God with you too."

This is why physical visits bring more comfort. Texts and notes have their power and particular purpose, but there is something about physical presence that brings added awareness, unity of purpose, clearer communication, and strengthened relationships.

Think how I must feel when someone comes to see me and brings God along, who seems to be saying, "Shelly, I am right here with you. I am perfectly informed of your situation. I am going to get you through this. I am hearing and responding to all your needs. You are my daughter. I love you."

Their presence *is* the gift. I wish I could say it more clearly. God is always with me, but when people come, it's as if He is more obvious, unavoidably so. I cannot mistake Him or doubt Him. A literal host of messages are conveyed when caring individuals step through my door—all without a single syllable being uttered.

Immanuel means "God with us," and it isn't a symbolic title to me anymore. I have stopped looking skyward for God—now I simply look toward those who come to comfort me.

Day 126: The Gift of Others' Presence

AS I THINK ABOUT PRESENCE, I REALIZE THAT EVERYONE CARRIES A particular presence. The person with the strongest presence will control and set the atmosphere. Since everyone comes with a desire to comfort and support, my home is permeated with comfort and support.

I can sense others' presence so easily now. I can look across a room and almost read what they're feeling. That's why it doesn't matter if they come up and talk to me or not. I can see what they wish they *could* say or do.

To the people who turned away from me or were hesitant to approach me, it doesn't make me feel sad or isolated. I receive, in some odd sort of transaction, what you wanted to express but just couldn't quite do it. Where did this gift suddenly come from? I have never seen people like I do now—beaming and compelling, all their good intentions continually broadcasting. How could anyone misread these beautiful messages?

These messages are constant open windows offering me new views of God's attention to me. Some people are windows of heaven because they share the teachings of God—not by speaking about them but by doing them.

All these presences feed others' spirits. Some people have a funny or humorous presence. Some people have a kind, accepting presence. Some are industrious and active, some questioning and seeking, some calm and reposing, some attentive and watchful, and some inclusive and considerate. There are all kinds of presences. Yours can change just by your mindset. What you believe and feel emanates out from you, and it is always trying to connect or influence everyone in your proximity.

Presence is the spiritual clothing you wear—the light you radiate. Some people have such a strong presence that others are impacted by them simply walking into the room. The air lifts and lightens and a kind of excitement begins.

Day 13: The Gift of Cards

THE MAIL IS POURING IN. I AM RECEIVING CARDS AND LETTERS FROM people I have not heard from in thirty years or more. It's amazing how quickly the news travels and how far it reaches.

Every card is appreciated. I read each one and keep them all. I can still go back and look at these cards, as they are physical reminders of others' concern. I have lost most of the text messages; they have been erased by my phone service. The cards, on the other hand, are stacked in a metal basket that I purchased specifically for this purpose.

The expressions in these cards, most produced by Hallmark, remind me that even though an experience can be unusual, the feelings that accompany it are familiar. Feelings are universal and widely experienced. For instance, we each know what it feels like to be betrayed, or what guilt feels like, or loneliness, embarrassment, fear, sadness, or frustration. These emotions are what make us human.

A line from a poem that I memorized years ago rises into my consciousness: "Sometimes the thing our life misses helps more than the thing which it gets."[13] With it comes a ratifying peace confirming the truth of this couplet.

Not for the first time, I am grateful to my husband's grandfather for opening the door of poetry to me. He called it "the best words to think on." He was right. Poetry is very good material for defining an experience. It proves the universality of unique occurrences.

If I want to isolate myself, I can point to the unique aspects of my particular difficulty and rightly claim that no one has ever gone through this before. But if I want to integrate myself, I can claim the universality of the emotions that accompany this difficulty. The choice is always mine to make.

Day 14: The Gift of Journaling

A TENNIS TEAM I PLAY ON IS ESPECIALLY SUPPORTIVE OF ME DURING this tragedy. A few days after Brieson's death, the captain, Julie, and the cocaptain, Laura, come to visit me. They make an appointment and arrive right on time. I open the door and see them standing there. They're nervous—unsure what they might be required to do, how I might be feeling, or what I might need. But they come anyway. Again, the resolution and fortitude of this act is not lost on me. I invite them in.

We sit down and talk about the regular things that people ask: How am I doing? Do we know why it happened? Is there anything they can do? The team misses me and sends their best. They don't stay long, but it's a positive and pleasant conversation.

As they're leaving, Laura hands me a journal, leather-tooled with an owl embossed on it. I'm sure she has no idea that I have an affinity for owls because the word *owl* it's the middle of our surname, *Rowlan*. I tell her that and she responds with some amazement. In addition, Laura is completely unaware of how much I like to write. That's a side

---

13. Alice Cary, "Nobility," Poem Analysis, accessed Aug. 16, 2023, https://poemanalysis.com/alice-cary/nobility/.

of me she had no way of ever seeing or knowing. But she felt impressed to bring me a journal—with an owl on it.

Inside the journal, she has included a list of words to describe grief. She says, "When you're writing down how you feel, here are some words that describe grief to help you express yourself."

This gift was God-sent, but I didn't know it yet. I set it next to my bed with no particular intentions in mind. At this point, I'm still using the other notebook for my lists or scrawling things randomly throughout the pages.

One night I wake up from the strangest dream, and I reach to write it down before it escapes my consciousness. I pick up the owl journal. It's 3 a.m., and instead of writing down the dream, I start to write about my experiences at the funeral. From that moment, this journal becomes an antidote to my grief—a healing place to think through the unusual experiences I'm having.

Although I have numerous empty notebooks and journals sitting within easy reach of my bed and a laptop I write on every day, it was Laura's journal that got me to start recording the surprising gifts and miracles of this journey. This journal has both positive and negative things recorded within it, but I share mostly the positive ones because (1) they are the overwhelming majority, and (2) they are the insightful and healing ones. Looking back, I realize that the negative and gloomy pages were never discerning nor perceptive.

Day 15: The Gift of Generosity

CASSIDY, A WOMAN FROM CHURCH, CALLS AND SETS UP A TIME TO come see me. Cassidy's brother had unexpectedly died exactly six months before Brieson. I have always felt a sort of kinship with Cassidy. She thinks things out, she likes math, and she enjoys teaching—lots of the things I like as well. She isn't afraid to speak her mind. I look forward to her visit.

She arrives with gifts in tow. One is a framed picture of an infinity symbol. I love it. It's the perfect gift. Brieson likes numbers; I like numbers. It speaks to me on so many levels—an incredibly thoughtful and meaningful gift.

Because of Cassidy's recent experience with death, I can welcome her into a more intimate space with my thoughts and feelings—even reveal awkward observations and probe the uncomfortable matters. Cassidy examines, rotates things around, and gives alternate perspectives. The longer we talk, the more I feel her fitting things to my background, and I repeatedly get the satisfying punch of two fragments seamlessly interlocking into a bigger picture.

I share all kinds of insights and ideas with her, and she explores them with me. Nothing I say startles her into silence. I share one especially divergent thought that has been weighing on my mind.

The day following Brieson's death, Colton, another young man from the area, was in a car accident—a Thursday tragedy and a Friday tragedy. Many people knew both our families. These double tragedies were announced to numerous congregations on Sunday. Later I found out that in one congregation, a leader stood up and announced, "Brieson and Colton were in a car accident last week. Brieson didn't make it. Colton is in critical condition."

This had some truth yet was quite misleading. However, if you were in that room and went home that night and wrote it down in your journal, and a few other people did as well, and then someone found those journals, say, fifty or a hundred years from now, then it would look like a corroborated story. Several people with limited connection to us had established a historical fact. I wondered if this is how stories about Joseph Smith were started. In our day, when communication is almost instantaneous, there were *still* miscommunications and misunderstandings of what had happened. Just imagine two hundred years ago when communication passed person to person over long periods of time; the chances of getting it wrong increased dramatically.

Immediately after sharing this with Cassidy, I think, *What am I saying? Cassidy didn't come to talk about Joseph Smith—she came to talk about grief and death. Ugh!*

But instead of raising an eyebrow, Cassidy pauses and then adds a few of her own ideas on this topic. She realizes that this is something I want and need to share. As she's talking, my jagged glass cracks wide open, and I feel as if I have been granted entry into a hidden sanctuary: *Shelly, you are going to learn many things from this, and it won't be the things you imagine.*

A feeling of beauty descends on me, and my shoulders relax in relief. This was a needed conversation. It is such a rare thing for me to be understood so quickly, and not merely understood but accepted. There is nothing quite equal to the gift of understanding.

We probably give too much praise to people with Instagram handles and TikTok accounts and podcasts, even though we get many exceptional ideas from them. Because more valuable and more needed are the people that we seldom celebrate or give credit to—the ones who allow us to find ourselves by rebounding questions and ideas back to us until we are confident in our own thoughts and discover our own insights.

True generosity has little to do with material donations. It is actually more about providing space to others to be who they really are or who they are coming to be.

Day 16: The Gift of Forethought

BRIESON'S GRAVE SITE IS IN MY HOMETOWN, A SMALL CITY IN ANOTHer state. It's a week later, and although we've posted his obituary in the town newspaper, I'm expecting a crowd of perhaps only twenty or thirty, mostly relatives. The sky is drizzling, and a tarp has been set up over about fifteen chairs. As we pull up into the cemetery, the day begins with a sort of hellish feeling but quickly alchemizes into something holy.

I am taken aback by who arrives: people from Phoenix who have driven ten hours for this twenty-minute ceremony, people from my graduating class, people who are Brieson's friends from college, parents of my friends, relatives who live near and far. There are well over a hundred people in attendance. As I look around, a peacefulness spins itself around me like a silk cocoon, and something very like contentment spreads through me.

I had not put much thought into this part of the process, but others had. Nicki, my sister-in-law, brings individual roses for people to put on the casket in a touching ceremony. Jodi, my friend from Phoenix, has arranged an entire meal to be prepared for all those in attendance. Buildings are scheduled, food is prepared, poems are read, pictures are taken, thoughts are shared, flowers are purchased and displayed, prayers are given—and none of this is my doing. I have never had such organized effort taken for me.

It ends up taking almost a year for the headstone to be chosen and engraved. My mother calls several times asking when it will be done. When it's complete, Carissa and Fielding, my daughter and son-in-law, take on the responsibility of tending to his grave site. They edge the marker, clean out the grit, and buy and arrange the flowers, always sending me a picture when they have been to visit. Others send photos of his grave site as well. Whenever I receive one of these pictures or texts, something deep inside me chimes with affection.

Day 19: The Gift of Confirming Stories

MELISSA, A FRIEND FROM CHURCH, SENDS ME AN ARTICLE TODAY about another mother, Heidi Swapp, who lost a son to suicide. I begin reading it half-heartedly, expecting it to be about grief and how grief feels. Instead, the article says this:

> "As the sun was coming up, I distinctly heard and felt the spirit tell me that a loving Heavenly Father had allowed Cory to come home," Swapp remembers. "And that thought has carried me. I knew that a loving Heavenly Father knew what Cory was going through and that Cory was not alone, that he was not off wandering somewhere, that he was going home.
>
> "He was going home and he was being received there by people that knew him and love him. And that every ounce of care that he

would need, he would be given and from that moment, I knew that we were being supported fully by heaven."[14]

My glass grows reverent. I experience an array of beautiful emotions. Finally, there's some confirmation that others have experienced what I have—not just the empty devastation but the loving messages. I look at the article. It was written today. Melissa must have read this and immediately forwarded it to me. I realize how much I wanted verification that the showers of tender mercies I am receiving—these divine messages—are not my own imagination or my own attempt to wish this away.

Day 20a: The Gift of Blending In

TODAY I HAVE A SEMI-PRIVATE LESSON WITH JOEY, MY TENNIS PARTNER. We arrive early and are the only people at the facility with the coach. Joey is gentle, generous, and positive; she always seems perfectly at ease in my presence, which is a gift by itself. As the hour progresses and the clubhouse opens, players begin filtering past our court. I can feel them pretending not to notice me. But ignorance and ignoring do not have the same posture. Ignorance is loose and unaffected, but ignoring takes exertion, and I can see them straining with the insincerity.

I wonder if I will ever be anywhere again without a kind of watchful formality descending. This must be what it's like to be a celebrity, except I am not well-known for anything people admire.

All this is running through my mind like white noise as I am hitting balls, and I'm hyper-aware of everyone hyper-ignoring me. I realize I did the same thing to Pam, and now I see how much easier it would have been to just acknowledge her.

During the drill, Greg, the coach, says, "Shelly, be careful! Move that ball that's behind you. You probably won't trip over it, but I want to be sure."

---

14. Morgan Jones, "Going home: Utah scrapbooking CEO finds hope after losing a child to suicide," *Deseret News*, Apr. 11, 2017.

I feel a zing—a full-out cleaving of the chest cavity. *That's what I have to be careful about—not letting the past trip me up. I can't be so worried about what's behind me that I don't move in the present. I can't let others' worries determine what steps I will take.*

After the lesson, Joey and I gather up our equipment and head toward the back courts for our team practice. Joey is laughing and talking with me. I feel confident at this point that no one is going to approach me. I push myself to accept that I will never be a part of this world again—not really. There will always be something slightly foreign to me from now on, something all these tennis friends will skirt around, pretend not to see, and avoid with polite deference.

But as we move across the court, Ron strides right toward me, without hesitation, making intentional and sustained eye contact. "There's our girl!" he booms. "How are you?" His voice carries across all the courts. He isn't afraid to acknowledge me or speak to me, just like he always has. He then gives me an engulfing hug.

I have to fight to keep from betraying myself. The last thing I want to do is burst into tears, heightening the awkwardness and increasing the uncertainty of everyone watching. His actions are in such stark contrast to the mental conclusions I have been building over the last hour that not even the most hardened pessimist could fail to recognize that I am at the mercy of some power higher than myself.

This power is always one step ahead of me, positioning covert agents with surprising messages to arrive at precisely the moment I hang in the balance. I think God probably smiles at that metaphor because these agents have always existed—I just never recognized their insignia until now.

I am filled with gratitude at this simple gesture. A gesture that would have meant nothing, literally nothing, thirty days ago is now permeated with the significance of acceptance. I guess when you feel like an alien, there is nothing you want more than to just blend in.

Day 206: The Gift of Particularized Plans

Julie, the tennis captain, understands my need for blending in and takes steps to make it happen. She gets the team together for a "practice." (We don't have team practices—ever.) She makes sure I will be in attendance. She has choreographed the smallest details. I learn later that before Joey and I arrive at the back courts, she has instructed the team, "It doesn't matter what you say, but you have to say something."

Virginia Pearce taught the same idea: "Learning to live with an open heart is not about learning to say the right words and refraining from saying the wrong words. In fact, just the opposite. I would venture to say that when my heart is open and filled with God's love, I cannot say it wrong, and when it is hardened and closed to Him, I simply cannot say it right, no matter how carefully I choose my words or phrases or inflections of my voice."[15] I found this true from the other side as well. As long as my heart was open and turned to God, I heard only the intent, never the words.

I am greeted by a gaggle of teammates who have prepared themselves to welcome me back. They begin with a group hug to get it over with as quickly as possible because they know I don't like hugs. And just like that, it's over—the awkward moment, the dreaded encounter, sliding past in a ripple of group acknowledgment.

Next, they ask me to present an award to Rona for being this year's "Head Cheerleader," a position we jokingly fight over. You might think they would do the opposite and present *me* with that award, but the irony is my exact form of humor, and I can't stop laughing because I often say, "Everything is always about Rona." This was a "welcome back" perfectly designed to kindle my humor and set me at ease.

Julie presents me with the team t-shirt, newly embroidered with "Mrs. Federer" on the placket. I am more than surprised. *How and*

---

15. Virginia Hinckley Pearce, *A Heart Like His: Making Space for God's Love In Your Life* (Salt Lake City, UT: Deseret Book, 2016), 64.

when did they get my shirt from my closet to do this? I ask several people. No one explains. I am beginning to realize the depth of planning that has gone on here; it has the feel of an architectural blueprint.

There is something about being a part of a group now that is so much more beautiful and appreciated—and needed. I have taken for granted, all my life, that I was one of the normal people. Finding this thread of commonality with others has new risk because I (and they) know that I am not the same. Every encounter is another test of whether people will accept this different me—this raw and gutted version of my former self.

I feel like a little bird with a broken wing that they are determined to mend. They gently pick me up and set me back in the nest, fully expecting me to fly again—and not a solo flight but as part of the flock, in unison with them.

It was not until later that it occurred to me to wonder how Julie knew to do such things. Where did she get this understanding? How did she know to do what she did? I felt fully a part of the team again, more at ease, and more included than I ever had. Julie made it all seem so natural. And, as you might expect, this entire experience won Julie my loyalty forever.

But she wasn't done yet.

Day 21a: The Gift of Reaching Out

JULIE HAS SCHEDULED ME FOR THE LAST MATCH OF THE SEASON "BE-cause she needs me." I know she does this to make me feel wanted. I could turn it down because I see it for what it is: I have become the team "charity case." I hesitate, and in that moment, my jagged glass pierces me so hard that I flinch: *Say yes!*

I silently enumerate the problems that could result from this endeavor, and there seems to be every reason to decline. The list is a long one and it ranges over wide ground, which includes the possibility I might burst into tears if I lose the match. This seems unwise in every way.

However, I don't have anything else to do, so I can't really say I'm busy, but I hedge a little. I ask who will have to play with me. As always, Julie anticipates my concern: "Lynette has asked to play with you." I don't doubt this for a minute. I'm sure they discussed and decided all the possible excuses I might give and have prepared for every one.

Receiving kindness of this nature is not as easy as it might seem. Receiving actually requires something of me; although it looks like a passive act, indeed it is not. Do I have the fortitude and reserves to engage with others for this length of time? Accepting this offering means exposing us all to the possibility of an emotional scene. Do I have the inner resources to accept this gift?

But Julie sees my need, and she isn't going to let it go unfulfilled. I place my heart in her hands and decide to trust her.

The match is over an hour away, so we meet to carpool. Julie puts only me in Lynette's car and shuts the door. I would think another person in the car would lighten the burden of carrying on a conversation with me, but Lynette seems unconcerned and handles the long drive perfectly, being chatty and at ease. I recognize the graceful strength this entails. Surely she must be wondering if I'm going to break down or get crazy or just refuse to talk. She doesn't know. I don't know. I am continually amazed at the pure moxie of these comforters.

Lynette and I win our match, but not without a little struggle. Then we sit on the lawn under a large, leafy tree and watch court two finish their match, which goes three full sets. Something about sitting on that emerald-green grass under those wide-spreading branches feels so safe. Time seems lengthened and lazy, like it once did in childhood. I want to stay like this forever, in this shady little spot.

Day 216: The Gift of Delivering

I COME HOME EMOTIONALLY EXHAUSTED BUT PHYSICALLY INVIGO-rated, an odd combination. I find that Tausha, another friend from church, has stopped by and left several interesting gifts on my porch. She texts:

I came by, check your porch. I've been thinking about you and praying for you. And feeling for you. The sign reminded me of Brieson, in his time here he sure made a lot of people laugh. That's how I will always remember him. And the plant because he loved gardening. And because Easter represents hope. And M&Ms cause they're good, lol. I love you guys more than you know. You are so special to me.

Another thing: I make shirts now as a lil business. I thought about designing a shirt in honor of him . . . with a pixelated something [I laugh—truly laugh out loud. She gets Brieson. I feel warmth flood up over me as I continue to read.] . . . something that he enjoyed (rake for gardening, earth for science, pencil for writing for example) and have a major amount of proceeds go towards something important. The science center, or some organization for depression, etc., lmk what you think. My heart is with you.

I close the text. Whenever I think of Tausha, I think of a special experience we had together in fasting for a blessing. And with fasting, the story of Esther comes to mind. Do you remember Mordecai's words to Esther? He essentially said, "Esther, you can keep silent, and God will send relief and deliverance by some other person. But who knows? You might have joined this kingdom for this exact situation." (See Esther 4:14.) Esther then devises a plan and takes courageous steps to comfort and deliver her people.

Like Esther, Tausha never backs down from an opportunity to make a difference. She seems especially invested in finding ways to serve me during this difficulty. She possesses a spiritual gift for crisis management. Or maybe it's better described as crisis artistry.

Sometimes we know exactly what needs to be done but don't have the courage to do it. Other times we have no idea what to do and a great desire to help. Tausha's gifts are the result of both desire and resolution (a form of courage). The sign, the plant, the candy, and the offer for a fundraiser are hard evidence of inspired plans and deliberate steps to comfort me through this crisis.

Even though I'm standing on my own doorstep in a perfectly safe and sunny environment, I get the strongest sensation of narrow escape and entering a secret refuge.

Day 22: The Gift of Ministering

ANGLEINA TEXTS TO MAKE AN APPOINTMENT. SHE HAS BEEN NEWLY assigned as my ministering sister, probably because she lives just around the corner. I wonder how she feels about this assignment. It can't be easy. She doesn't procrastinate though. She is right on top of it.

She comes alone, again gaining my immediate respect. We chat for a while. She is cheerful and kind. I assume that all we'll do is chat, but she has brought an article to share with me titled "When the Answer is Peace" (which I still have). It's obvious she has prayed and considered the best message to bring.

In the article is the story of Jesus falling asleep in the boat and the disciples coming to awake him and saying, "Master, carest thou not that we perish?" (Mark 4:38). Then Angleina hands me the article and has me read the following:

> How many times have I asked the heavens, "Carest thou not that [I] perish?" or "How canst thou lie asleep?" ("Master, the Tempest Is Raging," *Hymns*, no. 105). Perhaps the Savior could have just answered the question. That He cares. That the boat won't sink. But instead, "he arose . . . and said unto the sea, Peace, be still. . . . And there was a great calm."
>
> The disciples wanted to know if the Savior cared. The Savior gave them peace in the storm. When I've asked, "How come I have to deal with this particular situation in my life?" I don't usually get the answer I expect. And I probably wouldn't appreciate it if I did. If God answered all my questions with a spoken-word answer, it probably wouldn't always reach me or suffice my need. The facts of the matter aren't always what I need, even though it's what I think I want.
>
> Instead, "there [is] a great calm." The answer is simply peace.[16]

---

16. Liz Stitt, "When the Answer is Peace," The Church of Jesus Christ of Latter-day Saints, Apr. 14, 2017, https://www.churchofjesuschrist.org/inspiration/when-the-answer-is-peace.

My mind leaps away and starts mapping dozens of connections that have occurred over the last several weeks. A deep knowing settles inside me that God is indeed sending His Comforter, both directly and through emissaries like Angleina.

My glass feels ready to burst with energy. To my surprise, I feel my throat tighten, as if with tears, and I know something is coming. Then gently this is laid in my possession inside me: *All the things you have studied, Shelly—all the things you have pondered about death and life and angels and heaven—I am going to bring back to you now a hundredfold. You will understand them as you never have before.*

There is nothing I love more than learning about spiritual things. I seek this information constantly. I want to understand eternal doctrines, principles, and ideas. God is offering me one of my heart's desires.

I feel as if I have been admitted to some kind of library of transcendent studies with all the books on everything I ever wanted to know, leather-bound and brilliantly categorized with unlimited access.

Angleina gets up to leave as if this has merely been another visit of so many she has certainly made in the past. But this one will never be forgotten, and she has no idea what gift she has delivered: I am going to find my way forward.

Day 23a: The Gift of Fellow Travelers

IT'S LATE. I WENT TO BED HOURS AGO, BUT I CAN'T SLEEP—I'M NOT tired. Ideas and thoughts are running through my mind. No matter how I try, I am unable to quell the chaos rattling through my head. Gradually a light begins pushing away the darkness. This is more than a sensation—it's an inner picture, a vision, the slow opening of a curtain.

Then everything comes in an instant: a movie of events with an accompanying panoramic understanding—all quick but with perfect understanding. After the curtain closes, I bask in it for some time, trying to order my mind around what I have witnessed. As I do so, the happiness inside me grows and grows. I cannot contain it. I have to share this—express it.

I walk into the kitchen, open my Facebook account, and start writing. In one draft with a few tweaks, it's done. I reread it, push Post, then read it again. (See "A Few Weeks In: My Glass" on page 2 to see what I wrote.)

Before I have finished the second reading, Melissa, a distant friend, has loved it with a beating heart emoji. In that moment, I grasp something I have missed: I have joined an underground society—a world of silent sufferers. Melissa lost her father just a few days ago, and her heart emoji reminds me that there are dozens, probably thousands, of other pilgrims of grief, sleepless with sadness. This knowledge blocks some doubts and opens the way for hope to take up residence inside my heart.

I close the computer, walk back to my room, climb into bed, and fall instantly into a sweet and restful sleep.

Day 24: The Gift of a Blessing

A LITTLE OVER THREE WEEKS HAVE PASSED, AND NEITHER MY HUS-band nor I have had a priesthood blessing. One person did offer and then rescinded the offer when we said, "Yes, we would like one." Another person said he would not be comfortable doing so. Obviously, not everyone feels prepared to give a blessing in this situation, so now we hesitate to ask.

I decide to text a church leader who I briefly met several years ago and ask for his help. He expresses first surprise, since he had not heard of our son's death, and then sympathy, and he kindly offers to see us when he is next in Phoenix.

He arrives this afternoon with his wife. I have high regard for this man and know him to be a man of contemplation, kindness, and truth. He asks about each of us and again expresses his sorrow at our loss. He is remarkably calm, as though he has wells of tranquility to draw on and will patiently draw up buckets of water over and over until I am quenched. His poise and his tone, more than his words, seem to say, "I'm not worried, and you don't need to be worried either."

He then invites my husband, Stacey, to sit in a chair and gives him a blessing. I listen carefully to the words, and although they are beautiful and kind, I feel nothing in particular. Stacey rises and shakes his hand.

He then invites me to the same chair. I sit down. He begins. I am reaching out for something. I don't know what. What could possibly be said to me now that would make any difference to my state of mind and heart?

He advises me to pray for Brieson. "Even now, he needs your prayers." I am struck by this—of course, more than ever he needs the guidance of heavenly beings. Then he twice repeats, in exact verbiage, a phrase from my patriarchal blessing. It's not a common thing that's said, and he says it twice—just in case I think it's accidental or missed it the first time. Those four words push something out of my solar plexus. I spiritually relax, fully at rest, because a feeling I did not recognize was there is now gone.

A bliss such as I have never known swells up inside me. I feel hairs stand up on my forearms, and a small bolt of electricity runs down my spine.

I thank him, but my mind is whirling with things I need to remember. I want to push him out the door so I can ponder on all the things he has said, but hospitality dictates we chat for a bit longer. I am internally shaking because I am so anxious to get to my journal and write down all the things he has said and the feelings and ideas that have come with it.

Although the grief doesn't end with this blessing, it has changed shape, somehow becoming easier to lift and packaged in a more manageable form.

Day 30a: The Gift of an Eternal Father

I AM ON AN ELEVEN-HOUR FLIGHT TO EUROPE AND HAVE DOWNLOADed several books to read during this trip. My husband will be attending meetings all week in Germany, and I will need to entertain myself most of that time. By seeming chance, in one of the books, I stumble across the phrase "Eternal Father." This is not a new title to me—I have heard it literally thousands of times in my life and never blinked at it—but suddenly I can't read past it. Something stops me, inviting me to ponder.

Eternal Father? Why do we call Him that? An all-consuming desire to figure this out envelops me. I spend the next ten hours of the flight searching and reading everything I can on this title, this idea, this principle.

Eternity means "without beginning or end." Eternity encompasses time. God is Eternal, which means He encompasses and controls time. Time is within His power and marches to His orders. Scriptures tell us God has stopped the sun from setting or stopped the sun from rising, which are our foundations of time. Unlike the rest of us who bow to its relentless ticking, time has no effect on God (see Joshua 10:12–14; Job 9:7; 3 Nephi 8:22–23).

It dawns on me that controlling time is one of the greatest powers God possesses. *What if I could accumulate time? Save it up? Use it when I wanted it? Revisit the moments I chose? Or, even better, set my clock ahead through a painful experience?*

Perhaps that's a good definition of eternity: unending opportunities of time. Time will never run out. You will never be late, never regret something you missed, never make choices based on availability of time. The definition of time is the "apparently irreversible succession from the past through the present to the future."[17] That irreversible part is hard to swallow right now.

Perhaps this is why we often begin our prayers with "Our Eternal Heavenly Father." We really could say many things, but I have never heard anyone begin a prayer with "Our Omniscient Heavenly Father" or "Our Omnipotent Father." These are just as true as "Eternal," so why is that title so prevalent? Used as a modifier for the relationship of

---

17. *The American Heritage Dictionary*, s.v. "time," accessed Aug. 21, 2023, https://ahdictionary.com/word/search.html?q=time.

Father, it suggests something to me that every parent wants: to control time. Because controlling time makes everything you desire possible.

A soft and pliable feeling descends over me. *Shelly, I control time. I created time. Nothing is ever lost to me. I can rewind, fast-forward, pause, and delete time. I can shorten days or lengthen moments.*

My mind is spinning with all kinds of possibilities if time is not a factor. I can hardly still my mind enough to consider them in isolation.

Time moves one way: forward. I can't pause, go back, or even fast-forward. I must live through this life tick by tick by tick. But that is the mechanism for development. If I had the power to interrupt, pause, rewind, or skip ahead, I would probably never learn the lessons of compassion, patience, endurance, regret, and much more. It is the irreversibility of time that forces me to face my moral lessons.

If I were in charge of my own time clock, I would probably be tempted to go back and erase lots of things that only after years of living have I come to understand as beneficial. I've only realized the value because the clock kept ticking, waiting for me to develop enough character to understand the lesson.

My jagged glass is bouncing between my heart and my mind, prodding each one to higher levels of hope and anticipation. *You have not been robbed of time. You still have the same amount of it as you had before March 23rd—and so does Brieson.*

An Eternal Father has the wisdom to control time—to allow our maximum development. He also reigns in eternal realms, where there is no future and no past and everything is present. This allows unlimited possibility.

Eternity, and belief in it, is no small thing. It means I believe that nothing of this life is permanent or without recourse. It can all be made up because of the eternal nature of God. I feel and understand this more deeply than these words express, but I lack the vocabulary to express it effectively.

Day 306: New Realizations

I CAN'T STOP THINKING ABOUT ETERNITY AND TIME. THERE IS NO power I would rather possess at this moment than to be able to rewind time—slow it down. Or maybe I want to speed it up and get to the end of this life.

If I could go back in time, what day would I choose? Where would I start? I get the distinct feeling that if I were to go back and start over, I would still not be as happy as I think I should be.

As I think back over Brieson's life, I can't pinpoint a day or a time when the whole thing started to slide downhill. *Would I begin his entire life over again, trying to keep it from ending the way it did? Do I really have the understanding and capabilities to do that? What would I have done differently?* Even now I am at a loss of where it all started and why it all ended.

Although I have heard of people "living in the past," not until today have I considered what they really mean. Perhaps "living in the past" really means "wasting the present." The past cannot be retrieved, relived, or undone, which I know everyone would readily acknowledge. And yet if I continue to dwell only on the past, aren't I trying to do just that? Then my present becomes nothing more than a black and white, pixelated rerun—nothing new, nothing clarified, the same material churned over and over.

Right now, time has put me in a waiting room. In many ways I will never stop waiting through this life, looking forward to my re-union with Brieson. But I now see that as I wait, there will continually be people coming out from behind the veil to remind me that he is definitely being seen to. However, I still should not spend my days in the reception area.

Mourning is not problem solving—it's an act of creativity. This searching for *an* answer instead of *the* answer shifts and broadens my vision. Solutions require the right answers, but creativity requires asking the right questions. Grief is not a problem to be solved; there is no solution to what ails me. I don't forget it. It isn't changed. Instead, this research about time points me to a new set of questions about life, its purpose, and its meaning, and this leads me to hope for formerly unconsidered things like permanence.

Day 30c: Permanence

WHEN I STOP TO THINK ABOUT IT, I HAVE VERY LITTLE EXPERIENCE with permanence, and yet something within me seems to feel this should be the state of things: eternal, infinite, forever. Impermanence is the state of this world, and I can't remember any other way of living. Things come and go at an ever-increasing rate. We turn over almost everything in rapid succession—upgraded, the latest, Version 2.0. Nothing lasts forever, we say. So why am I upset by loss? It is business as usual in this world. Yet I seem to inherently know this isn't the way things should be—a fundamental premise of existence has been altered. I get a kind of sadness whenever I see something being replaced now, as if that's further evidence that this world is a hoax.

Day 32: The Gift of Interruption

IT's 8:30 A.M. AND I'M IN A HOTEL IN GERMANY. MY HUSBAND LEFT over an hour ago for work meetings. It is well below freezing and starting to snow. I decide that today I will finally tackle the question that looms in my recovery process. I get the sense that people believe I am in denial or trying to fake my response. Maybe I am. Today I am determined to find out. I commit to delving all the way into my feelings and seeing if anything surfaces that maybe I have been pushing away.

You see, ever since Brieson's death, I cannot think about it in a negative way. Every time I start into blighted or gloomy thoughts, two kinds of interruptions consistently happen.

The first kind is that some sort of mental door is triggered. Even if I am awake in the middle of the night and I start into a negative rumination, then something abruptly slams shut in my mind. Access denied. My thoughts are halted in midair. Then, quite gently, better and happier moments flow into my mind, all without any effort from me.

The second kind of interruption comes from others. Someone will text or call or drop by just as I am swinging the prison door shut on myself. Their communications often hand me a key, and the thoughts and feelings are easily released with a gush of newfound freedom.

These interruptions have happened so many times that I cannot dismiss them as coincidence. Yet at the same time, I wonder if somehow I might be subconsciously doing this.

Today in Germany, all alone in a hotel for ten or more hours, is the perfect opportunity to push through these limits because I know no one is going to interrupt me. No one will drop by. No one will knock. I need only grapple with the interior door.

But first I need to get some breakfast, which entails going down to the lobby to the free buffet. As I get dressed, I hear an incoming text. I wonder how I hear this across the entire room from a silenced phone. But when I pick it up, it's not a text—it's a Facebook message from Kevin, my Sunday School co-teacher. He is asking for help for another friend who lost a son. Kevin is planning to meet with his friend, and he wants to talk to me before he meets with them.

I tell him that I'm in Europe for the next ten days. I assure him that I am willing to help but not sure how I can. He responds that he didn't realize I was out of town but wondered if he could still ask me a few questions. One of his questions is "How are you coping with this?"

I startle when I read the question because this is the very thing I am determined to discover today: Am I coping or am I repressing?

Even though this is an interruption, it does not divert my thoughts. Oddly, he has asked me the very question that is on my mind. Maybe this is the beginning of dredging up the hidden emotions. I start typing:

How do I cope? That's the strangest thing of all this to me. I think God has taken this from me. I feel so much peace . . .

I don't know why exactly. Peace from the first five minutes of finding him. I am going to get grief counseling and also have kids

71

do it. It's on our mental health wellness plan. Pam and Dana said they also went to groups for parents who lost children. I guess so much comfort comes to me because of my study of near-death experiences, angels, and the plan of salvation. It seems from all accounts that the death experience is truly wonderful for children. They are met . . . immediately . . . by people they trust and know. . . . They meet Jesus. They don't miss earth. They are busy and happy and want parents and siblings to know they are well and better and happy. I told all this to my kids and they all feel it too.

As I'm typing, a very deep confirmation accompanies the words I am sending. I identify with them from a significant place within me. All the things I have learned about angels, the plan of salvation, and the afterlife come rushing through my mind.

We trade a few more texts back and forth, and I share with him my study of the word *eternal*. At the end of the conversation, I am sitting at a table in the lobby happily eating a bagel. The conversation has enlivened my glass, and I feel the full force of the next realization: *It's midnight in Phoenix.*

Why would Kevin message me at midnight if he thought I was in Phoenix? But I realize that if he had messaged me at a normal time of day, I would have been asleep in Germany.

I am fighting to keep my glass from showing me the truth, but I may as well have been trying to blot out the sun. Instead of discovering that I'm subconsciously sidetracking myself, I receive one more confirmation that God is controlling these interruptions. My breath hitches, dazzled by the brightness my glass is sparking.

My mind was on a one-way train this morning, and Kevin seemed to just run alongside the tracks and leap aboard—so casually and easily that it didn't feel like an interruption at all.

I usually get a change in trajectory, but Kevin's questions actually added fuel to my thoughts, burning the experiences into something instructive. He seemed to merely point out a wider vista, broadening and building on my own direction.

Later I read about the Apostle Paul who suffered so many trials yet understood the need for positive fuel. He tells me to think on things like prayer, gratitude, purity, justice, and virtue, and most importantly to think on the things I have received and learned, like Kevin prompted me to do today. It adds significance that Paul wrote this while in prison:

> And the peace of God, which passeth all understanding, shall keep your hearts and minds through Christ Jesus.
>
> Finally, brethren, whatsoever things are true, whatsoever things are honest, whatsoever things are just, whatsoever things are pure, whatsoever things are lovely, whatsoever things are of good report; if there be any virtue, and if there be any praise, think on these things.
>
> Those things, which ye have both learned, and received, and heard, and seen in me, do: and the God of peace shall be with you. (Philippians 4:6–9)

Indulging my thoughts on unfair or ugly things will merely push away God's peace and, with it, healing. Of course, there are horrible things to be met in this world—Paul knows this better than I do—yet he reminds me to think about the praiseworthy things in this world, and then God's peace will be with me.

I spend the rest of the day thinking and writing about the praiseworthy people in my life—people like Kevin and Jodi and Kathy and many others—so that I can add my witness to Paul's that this is the equation for peace and healing.

Day 34: Humming

WE HAVE ARRIVED IN ITALY. IT'S BEEN A LONG DAY: A BUS RIDE, A train ride, another bus ride, another train ride, and now finally one last bus ride to our hotel. I'm in my seat, leaning my head against the window, just staring out into the middle distance while waiting for all the passengers to board the bus. There is the usual scuffling and arranging and some muted conversations. Then a baby starts to cry. His parents are trying to quiet him and divert his attention, but he continues to whimper.

Suddenly a memory surfaces—a very vivid recalling of an experience. I am on the farm where I grew up. The day is sunny and warm, with a soft breeze blowing up from the creek. Maria (my sister-in-law), Brieson, Siearra, and I are walking through the field below the house. Brieson is perhaps six years old. The weeds are to his waist as we leisurely stroll through the field, and he is brushing his hand along their tops, sending all kinds of fluff and motes floating up into the air.

Maria and I are chatting, then Maria says, "Don't you love it when children do that?"

"Do what?" I ask.

"Hum. Like Brieson is doing. You know that when a child is singing quietly to himself, he is really, truly happy."

For the first time, I notice that Brieson is softly humming something—so quietly that we can't catch the words—as he brushes his hands across the tops of the stalks. He is fully immersed in the moment, engaged in nature, and taking in everything around him with curiosity and delight.

Back in the Italian bus, a satisfied gratification settles over me. Brieson is here with me, in Italy, humming.[18]

Day 36: The Gift of No Retreat

EVERY DAY STARTS AND ENDS WITH GOD NOW—EASILY AND EFFORTlessly. I don't have to remind myself to do it. I wake up to the feeling that He is leaning over the bed, and I go to sleep feeling as if He is tucking the covers in around me. He never seems rushed or impatient. I can simply sit in His presence and feel Him. I don't have to invite Him in or entice or struggle. He is already here.

---

18. "Try this: Hum your favorite song for the next 20 seconds. Now, don't you feel better? In fact, there's no better way to calm your mind and boost your spirits than by humming a happy tune" (Linda Wasmer Andrews, "Hum a Happy Tune for Wellness," Psychology Today, Nov. 21, 2011, https://www.psychologytoday.com/us/blog/minding-the-body/201111/hum-happy-tune-wellness).

I feel myself getting deeper into the heart of God. He has never stopped me from doing this—I have simply never taken the time to dwell there for long.

I read a few days ago that God will never give you a life that makes Him unnecessary. On further thought, I am not sure God has as much to do with it as I do. I want easy and secure.

I see that in the past I have spent considerable effort trying to figure out how to need God less. Now I am probing for any hold, the tiniest niche, to anchor more to His life, His words, His promises—the rock of my Redeemer (see Helaman 5:12).

With this experience, retreat has become impossible; I am dangling from a cliff. Yet in a way that is not quite clear to me, this is when the miracles began. After I thought I had removed myself from all possibility of divine intervention, I am handed, almost hourly, pitons, cams, and bolts of tender mercies.

These small, powerful anchors to my Redeemer are often unfamiliar and unwieldy yet vibrating with deliverance, relief, and rescue. God is the preeminent first responder.

Day 37a: Angelic Mornings

IT'S BEEN OVER A MONTH SINCE THE FUNERAL, AND EVERY MORNING, without fail, between 3 and 4 a.m., I am gently awakened to chiming, pealing bells. I can't hear them—I can only feel their thrumming vibration and with it a sense of being closely attended to, minutely watched by some kind of heavenly team of caretakers who are checking my vitals, carefully noting down observations, intently analyzing charts, and diagnosing my needs. I am filled with an emotion the exact opposite of homesickness—something 180 degrees from regret and traveling away as fast as possible is the best way I can describe it.

This diagnostic period quite often includes a wafer-thin thought being gently laid on my mind—something easily absorbed, comforting, and satisfying. Other times the treatment is simply a few minutes of a heart-swelling chorus. It's the best part of my day, and I am brought into it every morning without endeavor, just swept from the edges of unconsciousness and into celestial realms. This lasts for only a few minutes at most, usually less than a minute, but I am left with more than enough to consume. Then I slide back into a deeper, fully restful sleep.

These brief moments at the breaking of dawn fill a craving of connection and meaning that is so deep that nothing in this world can reach it, no matter how many hours or days or years I work for it. Instead of some terrible aching void, which maybe is what some people with uncertain faith might believe follows this life, there is an existence that is more solid and more gratifying than anything in this world.

Several years later, I discover that Elder Parley P. Pratt taught the following:

> When the outward organs of thought and perception are released from their activity, the nerves unstrung, and the whole of mortal humanity lies hushed in quiet slumbers, in order to renew its strength and vigor, it is then that the spiritual organs are at liberty, in a certain degree, to assume their wonted functions, to recall some faint outlines, some confused and half-defined recollections, of that heavenly world, and those endearing scenes of their former estate, from which they have descended in order to obtain and mature a tabernacle of flesh. Their kindred spirits, their guardian angels then hover about them with the fondest affection, the most anxious solicitude. Spirit communes with spirit, thought meets thought, soul blends with soul in all the raptures of mutual, pure, and eternal love. . . .
>
> In this situation, we frequently hold communication with our departed father, mother, brother, sister, son or daughter . . . whose affection for us . . . can never be lessened or diminished by death, distance of space or length of years. . . .
>
> With what tenderness of love, with what solicitude of affection will they watch over our slumbers, hang about our pillow, and seek to communicate with our spirits, to warn us of dangers or temptations, to comfort and soothe our sorrow, or to ward off the ills

which might befall us, or perchance to give us some kind token of remembrance or undying love.[19]

Day 376: The Gift of Valuing

HOURS LATER, I AWAKEN TO THIS WORLD. "IT'S MOURNING TIME," MY glass shrills. My first thoughts are of death and feelings of bleakness. There's an uncomfortable weight on my chest, and the jagged glass is thrumming along just below the weight between my heart and my lungs.

I don't know which one is making it hard for me to take a full breath—the weight or the glass—but I know the former is suggesting that I curl up beneath it, with the other demanding that I get up and move.

I wonder what powers this glass. It seems to run under its own authority, from a source outside of me, independent of me and yet dependent on me as well. That's why it has to wake me up—it has to get me going in order to illuminate things for me.

Nothing will be revealed or resolved without my efforts.

It jabs me. *Get up!* I edge myself out of the bed even though there is nothing to do and nowhere to go. There's minutes, hours, days, weeks, months, and years ahead of me, and not a single thing interests me on the horizon. I try to occupy myself, but today nothing sticks.

At 1:23 p.m., I get a Facebook message from Stephanie, a friend from church: "Have you ever read this before? What are your thoughts? I just came across it and think it just makes so much sense!"

I immediately open the document and begin to read. As I do, my glass blossoms with two gifts. First, I feel that I am a person with a valuable opinion—something to share. Stephanie is bolstering my esteem, which is a much-needed commodity during grief.

Second, the article is not about grief, dying, or mourning. It's about one of my favorite topics: the Fall of Adam. Now, to others it

---

19. Parley P. Pratt, *Key to the Science of Theology* (Liverpool: F. D. Richards, 1855), 120–122.

may seem like a burden to read and think about such a tangled topic. To me it is a gift. This sent me right back to my scriptures and notes to consider these new ideas and this additional perspective. I would never have done this on my own. I required someone to "assign" it to me. I have a great inner need for questioning and wondering. Somehow Stephanie recognizes this need and sends me something to ponder.

I am once again in awe of God's messengers—in this case a messenger through Facebook. I would understand if she doubted herself, thinking, "Shelly doesn't want to hear about this now. She has bigger things on her mind." But Stephanie responds to a prompting and sends it right over. And like so many before (and after) her, she gifts it to me with probably a passing shrug, never knowing the light it provided.

Day 43: The Gift of Connections

JODI, A LONG-TIME FRIEND, ASKS ME TO GO ON A WALK. WE SET OUT toward the hills behind my housing development. The sun is streaming, a breeze softly blowing; I feel entirely at harmony with it all, enveloped in infinite care.

Jodi has been part of nearly everything up to this point. She has visited, gifted, helped, texted, and baked. Just about anything someone can do for a person in grief, she has done it. When I think of the gifts I have given to others in the past, they seem like pretend or imaginary gifts, unlike the ones Jodi has offered to me, which, although mostly intangible, seem more real than anything I ever wrapped and set under a tree.

One of those intangible gifts is the sharing of spiritual insights. She is a careful and diligent student of the sacred—not just scholarship but discipleship as well. I share many spiritual insights with her, so I am eager to get her input on my new burgeoning ideas and experiences.

In many ways everything I need to know has been long ago studied and learned. I merely must apply them to myself. Of course, principles are different things when tragedy happens to you personally, not in a book, and in actuality, not in imagination. Therefore, I needed Jodi's fine-tuning feedback.

Jodi is a thinker and a doer. She considers things from all kinds of different perspectives. She is open to contemplating the unconventional. I have great respect for her spiritual impressions and applications. She walks her talk. I tend to receive new insights whenever I am with her, and today is no exception.

We walk and talk for over two hours. As we get back to the house, we are in the driveway and Jodi is walking toward her car. She turns back and says something about Brieson being aware of me. I agree and then add, just out of nowhere, "Right. Death cannot separate us."

We both stop abruptly, and our eyes meet. This silence felt like the heavy pause before a momentous plunge. Suddenly, an entirely new dimension of sealing power occurs to me—connections pinging around in my mind, drawing together things I have experienced over the last thirty days as well as doctrines and lines from ordinances.

A basic tenet of our religion is that if one has received the sealing ordinance, then death cannot separate those individuals. I had always viewed this in the context that after we all have left this earth, then we will be together in heaven. But now I see it differently. Brieson is sealed to me. I live those covenants. Death cannot separate us—even now, even when I am here and he is in another realm.

I immediately go into my room and look up the definitions of *separate*. As I scan down the definitions, I feel as I have just been moved to a front row seat. Not everyone gets a front row seat; it's a privilege. A premium must be paid for it, I guess because only there does one see the tiny details. From this seat, I almost feel as if I am part of the production. I am reminded again that I have a central part to play, right now during this time. Much depends on my role.

Brieson cannot be separated from me because of my temple sealing. I always knew this but as an elementary essay—now it became a doctoral dissertation in scope. Death feels like, and appears to be, a separation. But if death cannot separate us, then I should experience the opposite, right?

Separate is defined in the following ways:

- cause to move or be apart
- detached or disconnected
- distinction or boundary between
- leave another's company
- stop living together as a couple
- discharge or dismiss from service
- sever association
- to go in different directions

But if we are not separated, then we experience these things:

- united, together
- joined, connected
- linked, bridged
- attended, escorted, guided
- marry, live together
- retain, engage
- correspond, closeness
- alliance, affiliation

However, I already knew this from dozens of experiences. Death ends mortal life, but it does not end the relationship or the ability to communicate; it has merely changed the channels of communication.

It's as if there's a glass between us now, and like all glass, it is both transparent and dividing—a window of sorts that separates while still allowing a gossamer-type of observation.

I can press against the glass, feeling the brush of fine threads that signal that my words and actions are being witnessed by others. A cobweb of feelings and understanding radiate through me—so light and so fine that it is hardly there, and yet it is a connection as real as speech. I suppose some people might classify this as part of a wishful imagination, but it has an unpredictability that my own ingenuity lacks.

The interchange often goes in unexpected directions, happens at the strangest times and places, and originates from the most unusual sources. Often I want to extend the conversation but am unable to do so. Sometimes the communication is deep stillness or penetrating peace or defining confirmation. Even without words, I know someone else is at the other end of the line because I get a dial tone when the call has ended.

These moments are surprising because they bring clearer understanding of Brieson than I ever had in this life. He always had up shields, walls, and defense mechanisms. His attitude and his communication blocked rather than invited intimacy. These shields, walls, and defenses are gone now, and his intentions are purely to soothe me. Thus, all his messages come tinged with charm.

Elder Richard G. Scott explained, "Relationships can be strengthened through the veil with people we know and love. That is done by our determined effort to continually do what is right. We can strengthen our relationship with the departed individual we love by recognizing that the separation is temporary and that covenants made in the temple are eternal. When consistently obeyed, such covenants assure the eternal realization of the promises inherent in them."[20]

I do not know where I got the idea that if I didn't tell Brieson I loved him while he was mortal, then I had missed an irredeemable opportunity. It is not true. Brieson tells me he loves me every day, and I him—not in some arrow-shot-into-the-heavens kind of a way but very clearly, as clear as the ink on this page.

These moments are gifts, not powers. A spiritual gift is not a power. I cannot summon it or wield it of my own volition; it comes at the pleasure of another. I am not boasting. I realize these things are happening *to me* and not *from me*. I have as much control over them as I do over my height or my eye color.

I feel like this is exactly what Paul was trying to teach us when he said the following: "For I am persuaded, that neither death, nor life, nor angels, nor principalities, nor powers, nor things present, nor things to come, nor height, nor depth, nor any other creature, shall be able to separate us from the love of God, which is in Christ Jesus our Lord" (Romans 8:39–40).

---

20. Scott, Richard G., "How to Obtain Revelation and Inspiration for Your Personal Life," *Ensign,* May 2012

Day 44: Gratitude

HAVING DONE RESEARCH ON GRATITUDE STUDIES IN MY MASTER'S program, I know what I have to do: write letters of gratitude. I have already done numerous gratitude exercises over the last six years and learned that gratitude helps us to be aware of the blessings we normally take for granted. Gratitude also prevents the seeping tendency to perceive oneself as a victim. I have written letters of gratitude on many occasions, but this time it feels like a lifeline dangling from a cliff.

I spend several weeks searching for the best stationery (vellum), the best pen (Sharpie), the best envelopes (black), and finally an illustrative heading:

> You may not remember the time you let me go first, or the time you waited for me at the crossroads, or the time you fell back to tell me it wasn't that far to go. You may not remember any of those times—but I do. And that's why I was not surprised when you came for me and picked me up and set me in your saddle and said, "Today we will ride home together."[21]

This morning I begin, and for months afterward—even years, actually—I continue to write these notes. This is when the original list became indispensable. When I look at the list, it is overwhelming—hundreds of names—but I am determined to write something to someone several times a week.

It is a real struggle to express what I feel. This exertion is emotionally expelling for me; I examine feelings, ideas, principles, and people. I try to get out onto paper the manner in which they have affected me and what they have given. This is often exhausting, more so than I would have thought, but somewhere along in the process, contentment always begins to spread through me. At the end of a writing session, I feel God's pleasure, and there is nothing that feels better than that.

---

21. Adapted from Brian Andreas, *Traveling Light: Stories & Drawings for a Quiet Mind*, Goodreads, accessed Aug. 17, 2023, https://www.goodreads.com/work/quotes/157564.

It may sound strange, but I feel so much closer—more open—to the friends I write to than to friends I speak with or text. As I write, I think deeply about who each person is and what he or she has given me. I dwell on him or her in a very particular way, without interruption or distraction.

Here are some things I have learned about gratitude:

1. *Gratitude is an act of healing.* As I think about what others' actions have done for me, it's as if frost is wiped from the glass. Ah! Now I see that it has been you all along. The healers are not unfamiliar but often overlooked.

2. *Gratitude helps me grow the beauty of the world.* The more I look, the more I see; the more I see, the deeper I feel; and the deeper I feel, the more I look. It is a perpetuating cycle. The fear disappears and the splendor appears.

3. *Gratitude fully absorbs me and transports me.* While writing, I feel a deep connection, almost as if I were somewhere else entirely—a place completely at peace. This vacation from the burden of grief is refreshing.

4. *Gratitude is a form of acceptance.* Gratitude sculpts grief, changing its architecture bit by bit. It allows me to embrace a chapter of my life that I had never envisioned nor wanted. But when I recognize the blessings hidden within the tragedy, I am better able to assemble the pain and the hurt.

5. *Gratitude attracts tender mercies.* An open heart is a tender heart, and God's small seeds of compassion are firmly planted in that soul soil.[22]

6. *Gratitude is the practice of seeing as God sees.* I am invited to a wider perspective of other's motives, desires, gifts, and characteristics. God is a generous giver. Sometimes I have judged His gifts by their covering, but gratitude requires that I open them up. Then,

---

22. President Dieter F. Uchtdorf said, "I have learned that there is something that would take away the bitterness that may come into our lives. There is one thing we can do to make life sweeter, more joyful, even glorious. We can be grateful! It might sound contrary to the wisdom of the world to suggest that one who is burdened with sorrow should give thanks to God. But those who set aside the bottle of bitterness and lift instead the goblet of gratitude can find a purifying drink of healing, peace, and understanding" ("Grateful in Any Circumstances," *Ensign* or *Liahona*, May 2014, 70).

without fail, I find beneath that wrapping a glowing brilliance. Everything that appears to be a trial, a sorrow, a duty, or even a punishment envelops a brilliant principle of heaven.

7. *Gratitude comes from recognizing the transitory nature of things.* Permanence inspires trust. Permanence says it has always been there and always will be there, so you can rely on it. But permanence also sometimes produces a lack of appreciation. Impermanence, on the other hand, has a way of propagating gratitude. Something or someone may not be here tomorrow, and our appreciation blooms. So many things that I have not paid the slightest heed to in the past are now saturated in beauty. For instance, there are no ordinary people—not one.

I find that these gratitude notes, which might be thought of as giving value to others, are actually teaching me to value the here and now. I am instructed to savor, this very moment, the depth of the tragedy. I never spent less than an hour on any note—sometimes three hours or more to get it close to what I felt. It takes less than a minute to read each one. The time levels alone indicate who has benefited and grown the most from these notes. Looking back, this was certainly the most beneficial means of healing I did for myself.

Day 51a: The Gift of Unrequested Blessings

I AM NOT ALLOWED TO THINK NEGATIVELY ABOUT THIS EXPERIENCE. You might believe this is a sort of denial of the circumstances, but it isn't. This has now occurred so many times, hourly almost, that I myself am baffled about how to explain or give merit to the power of it.

Just this morning I was thinking, *If pure, raw desire could call down answers from heaven, then Brieson would have risen whole and complete the moment we both saw him.* There could never have been a greater desire and a more sincere petition to heaven.

Immediately my mind is erased, and then the blackboard flips to a completely new thought—one I have never considered in all my life.

Very abruptly, almost sternly, I am given this thought: *Shelly, what are some things you have never asked for but were given to you anyway?*

I am captivated by this idea. Into my mind pours the multitude of acts that others have offered me. I did not ask for any of the gifts, texts, emails, support, love, attention, kindness, service, or help—any of it—that came streaming in as if from the very windows of heaven.

I didn't request any of those things, but God sent them anyway.

I climb out of bed and pull out my notebook. Turning to a fresh page, I write, "Things I have never asked for but which God sent to me anyway." The list flows easily. As I look back across my life, almost without exception, the things that I truly appreciate and value are things I have never asked for, but God just handed them over to me.

As I ponder the list, I begin to sense the lesson. Why would I assume God is denying me something now? I have many times in my life been frustrated because God was not giving me what I thought I wanted, needed, or deserved *when* I wanted it and *how* I wanted it. But all the time God was carefully choosing, packaging, wrapping, and sending gift after gift to me—gifts that I would open and use, then go right back to wondering why God wasn't answering my pleas.

Day 516: The Gift of the Unexpected

MANY PEOPLE HAVE COME WHO I EXPECTED TO COME. THEY ARE THE scaffolding that holds me up during this time. Some people who I had expected to rely on did not show up. I felt their absence. But the people I cannot get out of my mind are the people who I hardly know who have reached out to me. The strangest assortment of people has entered my life—exceptional people.

These people are not easily explained. They are not people who have suffered a similar loss or people who knew Brieson or even people who know me that well. But these people, with their simple texts or emails and short comments to me in person, always brought me up sharp and quick because their message was so clear: *God is watching you. He sent me. You are remembered.*

Because why, oh *why*, would they come? I am baffled by their responses. I know that the human thing to do is to turn away from me. I understand that response perfectly. It's the one I would (and did) do, with the idea that the grieved person needs time and space to heal. But these people—these anomalies who had no responsibility or expectation to come—came anyway. I would never have noticed their absence, but when they came it was like lightning to me.

This only makes sense to me if they are sent. They may not even see it themselves that way, but their behavior is so abnormal that I cannot explain it any other way. To others, and even to themselves, they might have appeared small on the surface, but each carried a depth of significance known only to me.

Here is just one:

Dear Shelly,

I just wanted to send you a letter to let you know I am thinking of you and your family. And I am sending prayer and love your way. Since our first Sunday in our ward you and Stacey have been so friendly and welcoming. I am so impressed by how you serve and include everyone. Your example and love for the scriptures has really touched me. I was always enlightened and uplifted by your Sunday School lessons. I cannot even imagine the emotions you feel right now. But I wanted to let you know that you have made an impression on me, you have made me feel loved and have taught me. So in this difficult time, please find some relief in knowing how you have lifted and been a light to so many people. You are special.

Sending love and thanks,

Heidi

I read this note over and over. In many ways Heidi is describing a long-forgotten person. I hardly remember this person. But her sentiment brings a sharp piece of light.

I cannot list all the people who did this. There were so many mini-mighty moments, tiny-Titanic instances, of unexpected people reaching out to me that to list them all would be impossible. But every single one was piercing.

Day 54: The Gift of Prayer

DOZENS AND DOZENS OF PEOPLE TELL ME, "I AM PRAYING FOR YOU." This is somewhat of a social convention. I realize that. Still, it is the best thing to say. It really is—especially if you mean it.

This accumulation of heavenly petitions offered at unknown times by unknown people allows me to feel God saving me over and over. I now recognize this as the soft breeze that blows through my day, something easily overlooked or dismissed if my attention is not on it. But when I watch for it, I can effortlessly acknowledge the direction from which it comes.

I know we were the subject of many people's prayers, but today in the mail I receive a gift that surpasses all others.

Iris, one of my young women from years ago, writes me a letter. She shares some sentiments with me, and then she says this: "I promise to pray for you every day for an entire year."

I know Iris, I know her character, and I know she will do it. I know that Iris has not made this promise rashly. She has considered and pondered what she can do—what she can commit to do. She is so serious about this commitment that she writes it down, signs her name, and then mails it to me—all the elements of a legal contract. She is helping me with her understanding that this will not be over for a long time, and she is here to support me through it.

I know enough about heaven to know that prayers set things in motion. God will not overrule agency. Angels come when bidden and invited. What an incredible gift to know that someone is setting heaven in motion for me every day.

I realize how little I have relied on prayer in the past, kind of using it as a last-ditch effort when all other actions have failed. Now I see prayer as the power boost to get the assistance started and sustained. Many wanted to help me by doing something relevant and making an immediate impact. But this gift of Iris's is a tender discipline that I can already feel laying bricks inside of me, building me up, and protecting me.

Day 59: The Gift of Nevertheless

IT'S SUNDAY MORNING AGAIN, AND WE ARE AT CHURCH, SITTING ON our usual bench on the third row. Jeff, a member of the stake high council, arrives to speak. He nods as he walks by us on the way to the front.

The bishop gives all the preliminary business, then Jeff begins his talk by saying something about feeling welcome in this ward and that he knows many of the people here personally. Then, for a reason I cannot explain, I know he is going to say something about me. Without him turning his head or making any eye contact, I feel it coming.

"There are people here who have impacted my life in many ways, some with only a single word." I knew what he was about to say. It was more than a premonition; it was certain knowledge.

He continued, "I will tell you what the word is: *nevertheless*."

That single word downloads platoons of power into my heart—not just strength but also strategy, with the full understanding laid out with military precision.

Jeff is reminding me of a testimony I shared over twenty years ago in a stake conference session. I am stunned that he would remember it. I had once studied this single word for hours, searching everywhere to understand its application.

The only time the Savior seemed reluctant to obey God's command was when He was in the Garden of Gethsemane. Jesus was beginning to realize what suffering for all the sins of the world might require of Him. He said, "Father, if thou be willing, remove this cup from me: *nevertheless* not my will, but thine, be done" (Luke 22:42; emphasis added).

I had not thought about this in years. My previous research on this word had taken me to the Book of Mormon where I discovered that Nephi also used this word in difficult circumstances. Nephi would explain a challenging situation in his life, a legitimate struggle, and then instead of using this difficulty as an excuse "to be less," Nephi would say "nevertheless" and obey. This word seemed to work as a transition from doing his own will to following God's will.

As Jeff continues to speak, I begin to recall the list of answers Nephi gave. I had once known them completely by heart, but now I can remember only a few:

- "Having seen many afflictions in the course of my days, *nevertheless* . . ." (1 Nephi 1:1; emphasis added).
- "Being exceedingly young, *nevertheless* . . ." (1 Nephi 2:16; emphasis added).
- "Not knowing beforehand the things which I should do . . . *nevertheless* . . ." (1 Nephi 4:6–7; emphasis added).
- "They did treat me with much harshness; *nevertheless* . . ." (1 Nephi 18:11; emphasis added).
- "Great was the soreness thereof. *Nevertheless* . . ." (1 Nephi 18:15–16; emphasis added).
- "Thou hast suffered afflictions and much sorrow. . . . *Nevertheless* . . ." (2 Nephi 2:1–2; emphasis added).

No one gets to choose the trials of their life; I can only choose whether I will follow my own will or God's will. However, I will not be doing this alone. I am part of some heavily armed and highly organized celestial ops unit, authorized because of particular training to meet this unique difficulty. Nothing will be compromised. They merely await my verbal go-ahead.

Sitting in that chapel, looking down at my hands, I whisper, "Nevertheless."

Day 60: The Gift of Support in Daily Tasks

AS THE DAYS TURN INTO WEEKS, AND THE WEEKS INTO MONTHS, I realize I can make this easier or harder on myself. Mourning is often a Sisyphean endeavor. No matter how well I pushed the boulder up the hill yesterday, today I have to wake up and do it all over again.

I soon discover there are some things that help the process and some things that hinder it. As usual, I make some lists. First, I note things that seem to make the day go better, such as the following:

- **Get up, shower, and dress like I am going somewhere.** This puts me in some kind of optimal zone.
- **Play tennis regularly.** This takes my mind off everything and gets my adrenaline going—a natural mood booster.
- **Go outside and be in the sun.** Nature has a nurturing effect.
- **Write letters of gratitude.** This broadens and builds my awareness of others' efforts in behalf of me.
- **Create something.** I often don't have energy to finish it, but the effort pulls my mind away for a time.
- **Journal or write honestly.** This helps me analyze the things happening interiorly.
- **Be with people for a period of time each day.** This helps me feel belonging.
- **Be alone for a period of time each day.** This helps me process new experiences.

I also discover there are things that don't help me. Now, I realize these selfsame things might be restorative to others, but to me, they are not. That's the value of creating my own individualized list—I can contemplate and recognize my own prescription and instruments of healing. This list included the following:

- **Lying in bed past 9 a.m.** This, more than anything, undermines my joy and thwarts revelation.
- **Reading fiction.** There are some exceptions, but this is surprising because it's one of my greatest hobbies. But this became an exercise in frustration—I could hardly go twenty minutes without feeling futile, which is why people who send me articles to read are a blessing in mindset. Of course, looking back I can see that I probably wasn't reading much because all learning was coming from the inside out.

- **Posting on social media.** This keeps me going back to that site looking for "likes," and it soon spirals me into a feeling of emptiness.
- **Having no plan for the day and just meandering about.** Even one project or thing to accomplish that day has a great effect on my entire mood.
- **Studying the plan of salvation.** This is also very odd because my beliefs in it have not changed—at all. In fact, I know things more clearly now than I did before. But somehow, the study of it seems like reading kindergarten books—too elementary, too narrow, too frustrating.
- **Being at parties or large gatherings of people.** I often feel swallowed in anonymity and carefully avoided.

Now, you might think that because I have crafted this list, I would never do those things that are detrimental, but it doesn't always work that way. Grief knocks me around, and I have to work to get on top of that feeling. Then I can usually hold it at bay. But climbing up and over grief also means there is the possibility of falling off it. Sometimes I lose my footing at the most unexpected times, and down I go.

At that point, it just feels good to lie there under that boulder. It brings a certain sense of empowerment knowing that I'm at the bottom of the pain—and still breathing.

Even knowing something is beneficial for me, sometimes I just can't generate the energy to do it. But if someone else asks me to go for a walk or take a class or go to an event, even if it only lasts thirty minutes, it affects my mourning capabilities for several days in succession. Anyone who helped with things from the good list, even unwittingly, aided in my healing.

Day 62: The Gift of Unwearied Diligence

WHEN BRIESON'S YOUNG SINGLE ADULT (YSA) BISHOP CAME THROUGH the receiving line at the funeral, I recognized him and thanked him for all he had done for our son.

He replied, "I didn't do enough."

I was taken aback. That is not how I saw the situation at all. I was fully convinced that he did everything he possibly could. He gave more than I had even hoped.

Today this moment flashes over and over through my mind, as if the glass is trying to bring my attention back to it to really see it. I keep turning away from it until a thought flickers through my mind: *The YSA bishop's service, although aimed at Brieson, was also for you!*

When this thought solidifies, my piece of glass pulses in confirmation. All that was done—all that seemingly useless effort—had a dual purpose: so I would know that someone was trying—that God sent someone.

This verse rang inside of me like a church bell: "Inasmuch as ye have done it unto one of the least of these my brethren, ye have done it unto me" (Matthew 25:40).

One? I thought. *One of the least? His works done for Brieson were done for me?*

This YSA bishop had never met me. We texted and talked on the phone once. He had no reason to respond with such alacrity to my requests that he help Brieson. There was no previous relationship, no debt or obligation. This bishop gave only with pure desire to help Brieson.

The glass traces a line of lights across my inner expanse, showing me that God was aware and watching over me long before I would be in this place, in this very moment. Because of this bishop, I could never say, "If only someone had reached out to Brieson."

Because someone *did*—and that knowledge meant more to me in this moment than I thought it ever could. I feel it prickling all along the back of my neck, the way hair sometimes rises in a lightning storm.

I remember another incident that happened the Sunday before he died. By chance, I parked next to a member of the YSA bishopric in the parking lot. I was leaving; he was arriving. As he got out of his truck, he asked about Brieson. He said they had been talking about him in ward council that morning and that he was going to reach out to him.

I warned him that Brieson probably wouldn't answer his texts. He replied, "That's okay. I'll call anyway."

To know that while Brieson was on this earth, someone else cared about him, someone else thought about him, someone else talked about him, someone else worried about him, someone else made plans for him, and someone else gave time to him—these are gifts without price and which cannot be given posthumously. No matter how much someone might think about him now, it cannot compare to those who thought about him before his death. It is a pound of granite to a pound of feathers—both of the same weight, but only one can be the foundational support of heavier things.

The value of this gift only settles on me today, months later. As I contemplate these actions, their worth grows. I was not privy to all the interactions they had together, but I am certain that Brieson consistently rejected this bishop's offerings, pushed away his suggestions, and made things difficult in general. But this bishop and others softly persisted.

Did he do enough? I can answer that with a full, resounding "Yes!" He gave when there seemed to be no reason to do so. He continued despite futility and rejection. He offered with pure intent. Sometimes efforts of this nature are not appreciated for years, and when finally seen and recognized for what they are, they carry astounding feelings of attachment. I speak from experience on this one.

My jagged glass pulsed and paused until I felt the full force of the gift this bishop and counselor had given us and saw it for all that it was: the long wrestle of securing promises. Just as Jacob struggled through the night, never yielding, until God's blessing was granted—a promise that affected not only himself but generations of people—these men's determined efforts have blessed me (see Genesis 32:24–26; 35:11–12).

I need to build more understanding in the priesthood's ability to effect change on both sides of the veil. After all, it is a key element of priesthood power and authority (see Matthew 16:18–19), both of which this bishopric offered to Brieson with unwearied diligence (see Helaman 10:5–11).

Day 66: Midnight Messages

I WAKE UP AT 3:30 A.M. I'M WIDE AWAKE, LIKE BEING PULLED IMMEDIately from a deep sleep to crashing sound.

But there is just stillness—the quiet and darkness of rest. So what has woken me up? There's a pause while I collect my thoughts, and then . . . pure joy.

I am infused, saturated with an accelerating joy, and consumed by it.

But there is something else—something very fragile just at the edges. It feel like the tenderness of someone watching: Brieson. He is so pleased—so excited about something that he has woken me up to tell me.

Tell me what? What has happened? There is no answer, only a pulsing sensation of sheer joy. I am simultaneously serene and celebratory for no reason I can name.

Is that possible? Doesn't something have to happen in order for this level of excitement and anticipation to occur?

I lie in bed and bask in it, wondering what this could all mean. I search my mind for some link—some message to greater understanding. None comes. No voice. No idea. Just this joy.

Maybe I can still have happiness. Real happiness. Perhaps March 22nd was not the last happy day of my life.

The silence is velvety as it settles across my mind, quieting and pulling things away from me and letting me sink back to sleep. No weights, no prickles—just lapping undulations.

Day 68: The Gift of Beating Hearts

MY GLASS DOESN'T WAKE ME UP TODAY. I TEST IT A LITTLE BY PUSH-ing myself to feel more sadness. Nothing—just a weight in my chest. I burrow further into my bed, expecting a sharp jab, but still no re-sponse. I'm surprised. The glass has never let me down before.

I roll out of bed mostly from habit, get vertical, and start the routine.

I need some inspiration—some contact today. I once imagined that lying in bed and thinking it all through would be the most pro-ductive way to reach outer realms, but not always. Sometimes I have to get up and get going. I guess today is one of those days—just letting my mind search and my heart feel.

I look outside. It's a perfectly sunny, beautiful day. Before I can feel myself out of it, I put on socks and shoes and head out the door. I don't want to go walking or even be outside, but history has shown me that sunshine and exercise will exorcise the demons that flourish in shadow and lethargy.

I walk on a dirt path just north of my house along a canal. I have taken this walk dozens of times. I am not here to see anything new; it's all familiar territory. I am looking down at the ground mostly, just putting one foot in front of the other. Then something whistles and I look up as a thought is gently placed in my mind: *The widest conduits for revelation are courage and diligence, and both require exertion of the heart.*

That's it—just that one sentence—and I am given a moment to ponder it.

More ideas flow into me*: Your beating heart clears your mind. The more beats you can get, the clearer your mind.*

My heart is certainly performing at peak levels all the time now; I am just trying to keep it at a steady beat most days. Does an erratic heart have benefits?

I already knew that the mind and heart are involved in revelation, and I also knew that endorphins were part of exertion. I had never considered that a hard-beating heart clears the feelings, frees the intellect, and opens a concentrated avenue for revelation.

In the depths of this tragedy, God was teaching me something I had always wondered about and studied for hundreds of hours of my life: How are the heart and mind related in revelation? Today, God just handed me something new.

He also added this caveat: *Don't stay in bed—I can't help you there. Get up and get your heart pumping. I promise it won't break.*

The more I thought about it, the more I realized that courage is a fundamental element of revelation because revelation will be tested. I can receive truths but then hesitate to act on those truths until I feel that "safe conditions" are met. If I fear acting on the truths I receive, then I deny both the Spirit and the message. Displaying divine truth in this world is risky, so courage is a necessary virtue of those who receive it.

Diligence is necessary because the more I think and feel about something without acting, the more my resolve is weakened. The more I feel without acting, the less I am capable of acting, and over time, the less I am able to feel. Acting without delay builds and refines my thoughts and feelings. God is teaching me that my ability to receive revelation is based more on character traits than conversation skills.

Day 73: The Gift of a Faith-Filled Journey

THE LESSON IN SUNDAY SCHOOL TODAY IS ABOUT THE THREE DEgrees of glory. We begin by reading this verse: "And now, after the many testimonies which have been given of him, this is the testimony, last of all, which we give of him: That he lives!" (Doctrine and Covenants 76:22).

The teacher asks, "Why do you think Joseph Smith says this *before* he even describes the vision he has had?"

In that moment, my glass thins to fiber optic, transmitting 25,000 messages at once. I see it all so clearly and so easily. We don't even need to go through all the verses—all the verses I know will be read—because I see the whole crux of the matter: being valiant in our testimony of Jesus Christ. To put it simply:

- No faith in Jesus Christ in the premortal world = sons of perdition
- No faith in Jesus Christ in the mortal world = telestial kingdom
- Faith in Jesus Christ until life gets difficult or we are tested = terrestrial kingdom
- Valiant in our faith in Jesus Christ until the end = celestial kingdom

Our entire future depends on our faith in Jesus Christ, which is why Joseph and Sidney want us to know that He lives! It's all real. There is a plan—a plan more intricate than can be described or explained and certainly greater than we can imagine.

I realize that I voted for—in fact, shouted for joy about—the opportunity to have a faith-filled journey. I believed in Jesus Christ and His ability to redeem us—all of us. I was excited to prove my faith in Jesus Christ.

I quickly look up the word *valiant* to find that it means "exhibiting or carried out with courage or determination."[23] When I read the definition, into the farthest reaches of my heart and mind comes an understanding so unequivocal I almost shout it out. My lens widens and the landscape of this life comes into sharper focus. *All of this—all of it—depends on my courage and diligence. We are here to be tested on those two attributes—the same attributes that bring revelation.*

My mind is whirling with connections. It takes courage to trust that even though most of our situations seem unfair and undeserved, it will all be accounted for in His plan. Nothing lies outside this plan—absolutely nothing.

All that is required for me to work that plan is to act with courage and diligence. Again, there's that pairing. I am being given so many

---

23. *Merriam-Webster.com Dictionary*, s.v. "valiant," accessed Aug. 17, 2023, https://www.merriam-webster.com/dictionary/valiant.

sweet gifts, with hardly any effort at all, as if I have tapped into some celestial database and it is simply transferring into my heart. The more I learn of this plan, the more irresistible it becomes.

Day 74: Looking Back with New Eyes

I HAVEN'T BEEN ABLE TO GO TO SLEEP. SOON MY MIND IS DRAWN BACK to Brieson. I don't try to push these thoughts away. I have never tried to push them away. I begin thinking about his childhood. He had some difficult social experiences in grade school, and I start to scroll through some of them. My heart begins a familiar aching.

THUD! A heavy door slams shut in my mind. I shake my head a bit to open it up, but the pressure is so tight that I can't budge it a single centimeter. I try to mentally drive through this barrier, but I can hardly squeeze a full thought through it. I stop pushing.

My awareness hovers there for a moment, then my glass sets a new set of lenses across my reflections. New memories are brought forward for my observation. These are the humorous incidents involving Brieson—and there are many. The memories are so vivid and proximate that it is as if I am experiencing them anew. The sweetest laughter bubbles up inside me. Stacey is asleep next to me, so I muffle the sounds by rolling on my side away from him.

For about a full minute, scene after scene flips through my mind, each one more amusing than the next as if I am building to the end of a comedic act. Then it's done, and the screen goes blank.

With a full reversal of my thoughts and feelings, I am left to consider what has just happened. I have gone from abject despair to stifled laughter in ten seconds. I don't have the capability to make this radical of an emotional change from my own volition—not that quickly and not that cleanly.

I begin to think of some of the most hilarious incidents of my own life and realize that some were quite painful in the moment, but now they are simply entertaining anecdotes. I guess not all pain continues to be suffered. Some injuries can become learning opportunities and even bond us to others, becoming almost medals of honor.

Tonight's message seems to be that Brieson doesn't see his past the same way he once did.

Day 82: The Gift of Pondering

I PLAY TENNIS FOR SEVERAL HOURS THIS MORNING. EVERYONE IS friendly and accommodating and we have some laughs, but then my insides collapse. I say I have someplace I need to be, and I pack up and leave. My bed is calling to me: the dark room, the familiar comfort of solitude, the need for privacy.

My thoughts are building up inside of me. Maybe with other people it would be emotions, but with me it's thoughts. And I know grief is waiting for me, pacing impatiently, filing her nails, flipping through magazines, checking her watch. I get home right as I hear my name being called. I slide into my bed and relinquish myself to her.

Grief doesn't make these appointments in order to torment; instead, it's necessary time for me to process and address. Grief is a coping business. Everyday things—common things, typical things—have to be reimagined and reframed. These small things must be examined in the new light and pitched to the new key. I must pay close attention to things going on inside of me—not just feel them but investigate them. Some things have to be slowly emptied out since my interior gets very crowded now. I need downtime—just time—to let God work inside me.

I have to make a great effort to stay in the exterior world. I am paying such close attention to every move going on inside of me. There are legions of things: earthquakes, tsunamis, eclipses, thunderstorms. Sometimes I wonder how anyone ever interacts with others since this interior takes so much climate control.

I once thought it would be the big events that would wind me up, but in the end, it's the small things that snarl my heartstrings—someone waving at me across the courts, a teen walking down the sidewalk hunched beneath a backpack, the lyrics from a favorite song.

Then each of those strings has to be followed from end to end, untangled, identified, notched, and tuned. Everything plays easier after

I have gauged each idea and strummed it in conjunction with what I already know. Some things for which I have no understanding seem to blend when placed between two things I have long ago learned. I consider and tweak until the ideas harmonize.

I use music as an analogy here because there's no greater emotional detangler than music. It smooths over the wild dissonance that stretched-out or broken feelings create. I have even made a playlist of songs that allow me to straighten out the strings, put things back into their proper scale, and get myself composed.

No matter how much support I have (and I receive a great deal), there are still times when I must carry this alone. Being alone doesn't mean I am lonely or isolated. This solo time helps me practice accepting my new path, my own strengths, and my own understandings.

Being alone is my time to rearrange ideas and think through new insights. This alone time actually helps me connect with others in a more authentic way because I am more comfortable with who I am and where I'm headed. This allows me to be confident in myself, which eases everyone, I think, because so many people seem to take their cues from me instead of the other way around. We talk of achieving closure as if this is a means of healing, but after these meetings with grief, I actually feel more openness to the events of life. I have lost my fear of so many things.

Day 98: The Gift of Compliments

I RECEIVED A LETTER TODAY (AND A GIFT) FROM MY COLLEGE ROOM-mate, Sandra. She had written a couple of pages recalling things from our past and things she thinks about me and hopes for my future. There were also some moments of bonding over mutual struggles. All in all, it was a heartwarming letter. I have received numerous letters of this caliber. The amount of time and effort that letter-writing takes, and the rarity of it in our present culture, speaks of great care and desire.

Every one of these handwritten letters is a manuscript of love. As I read through Sandra's letter and the very kind things she says, I realize how restoring honest compliments are.

Some people will counsel me about death or ask me questions about Brieson—really the same things other people ask or say—but somehow I get a feeling that something precious is being tarnished or that holy ground is being trodden upon. Other people, I think, want to flatter me out of sadness, throwing me adjectives and hoping one will be legitimate. Commendation of this kind is exhausting both to hear and believe.

But there is something potent about receiving a genuine compliment when someone recognizes something I have to contribute, pointing out that *I* am the gift—not just a cup of water presenting a single offering, but a continually flowing stream capable of giving so much more. That kind of approval reaches into my inner essence, healing without leaving a scar.

These genuine compliments cause my self-doubt to melt away. For hours or days, I can bask in them, my energy rises, my confidence springs up, and I feel like I have a purpose. And, more importantly, I am living that purpose.

In my former life, compliments were edifying to me. But now, during mourning, these words improve me. I am actually made better (recovered, healthier) when they are genuine.

Day 99: The Gift of Peace by Piece

THE LETTER SANDRA SENT ME YESTERDAY continues to hang with me today. The letter arrived with a quilt. Sandra is an avid quilter and designed this one with an astronomy theme and Brieson's name appliqued on the front. I can see that a great amount of thought and time was taken in piecing it together.

Sandra lived with me at a time when everything in my life was going amazingly well. I was engaged, I had just earned another scholarship, my grades were high, and I had been accepted to the School of Accountancy. I was happy, in love, and enthusiastic about the future.

When I look back, I feel even more like a failure, and I begin to blame myself for not being able to be the person I had planned to be.

I set the quilt aside and start to clean the house. I sweep the floor, fold the laundry, load the dishwasher, and (about seventy more times) only think about all the things that are never going to be. I wonder how things would have been different if I had made different choices. Better probably. I feel like scrapping the whole thing—brushing my whole past into the trash.

Eventually I end up back in my bedroom to find a pile of mail sitting on the chair. A bright blue envelope catches my eye, and I pull it out to find a card and letter from Lynette. In part, she writes the following:

> In attending Brieson's funeral, or better described, when I attended the experience of hearing the story of Brieson, I learned more about Shelly as well. You have five amazing, gifted, beautiful children. Brieson is so lucky to have had you as his Mom and part of his story. Anyone who earns a special place in Shelly's life is lucky . . . with you, I feel so fortunate to have found a truly beautiful person and a dear friend.

My glass aches once, hard, like an exclamation point typed at the end of a sentence. Everything sad ends on the dot. In an instant, I have a new peace about my choices.

I wonder why I didn't read this letter yesterday when it arrived with Sandra's letter and gift. Why did it sit here for twenty-four hours? I don't remember why I left half the mail unopened.

As I stand in my room holding Lynette's letter, I realize that I won't understand my life's purpose by throwing away the pieces. Each little shard or shaving of things that have happened—even those that don't seem to fit anywhere (the painful ones)—are needed to complete the full picture. Each moment of peace brings another interlocking piece of the puzzle.

Day 100: The Gift of Celebration

I DON'T EVEN CARE THAT TODAY IS MY BIRTHDAY BECAUSE I KNOW Brieson's birthday is coming up in a week. I usually plan some event, activity, or new thing to celebrate my birthday. But this year, I couldn't care less and have prepared nothing. But others do care and have prepared.

Bree, a lifelong friend, gifts me a glass tennis ball. I love the oblique reference to my Facebook post about carrying glass. It's a clever and perceptive gift as usual—Bree's trademark. I set it on my dresser, and every time I see it, I am reminded of my Facebook post.

Stephanie, a ministering friend, gives me tennis stationery and tennis wristbands. She doesn't play tennis and has never even seen me play tennis, yet she knows I would love both these items. They're uncannily personalized, and I am pleased with both and more so by her remembering.

My daughter Carissa invites me to a roller derby. She knows how much I love new and unusual activities. We drive all the way to Mesa and meet Terry and Nancy there—our friends who are always up for any adventure. The roller derby is an amateur league, and dozens of hilarious moments arise that begin with an audience volunteer incorrectly singing the national anthem and end with our picture next to a skater. We talk and laugh about it all the way home. This becomes a memorable birthday before we have even had time to look back on it.

We get home late from the roller derby, and I crawl into bed thinking how differently this day went than I had imagined. I have felt loved and catered to all day long. If nothing else, today taught me to live my life in hope—or maybe faith is a better description. Faith is simply the belief that the future will be better than the past, so you keep right on marching toward it, even if it takes you through fields of mud. If I choose to let go of my regrets and trust that this life (and my life, and everyone's life) is precious and meaningful in the eyes of God, then something new awakens in me, and something beyond my own expectations is sure to happen to me.

Day 108: The Gift of His Life Remembered

GRIEF HAS TENACIOUS TENTACLES. IT BURROWS AROUND INSIDE MY vital organs—my lungs, my heart, my mind. Most of the time it just floats along inside me like an accustomed visitor. But occasionally it will rear its head and wrap itself tightly around something nearby—and squeeze.

Sometimes I see it coming and sometimes it surprises me with its predatory swiftness. I know the constriction can't last forever, so I have gotten rather good at waiting it out. I completely suspend my breathing or pulsing or thinking until it relaxes, then I emerge back into this world.

I felt it stalking me today—on his birthday. It's agonizing to consider the future that will never be. All day long, lost future moments are slithering and constricting through my mind and heart. Brieson should be here.

Fortunately, like all creatures, grief is part of a food chain, and there is something that can devour it as readily as it gnaws away at me. So I wait it out, trusting that God will send out an hunter today of all days.

And He does. It comes in the form of my youngest daughter, a teenager.

For days Siearra has been working on a video to post on Brieson's birthday. Today she loads it up and then comes into my room to check that I've seen it. This video documents moments from Brieson's life and even a particular birthday. This has taken Siearra dozens of hours to create. As soon as she posts it, people begin to like and comment.

I watch it over and over. My feelings aren't exactly happy, nor are they sad—they are something else, though I cannot say what. As I click to start the video again, I suddenly can't hold back. I have to speak, out loud to God, at that very moment. It is either tell Him now or burst wide open.

"God," I whisper, "thank you for Brieson."

Siearra helps me remember the good times, and I feel privileged that I knew Brieson—*experienced* him. Every person is irreplaceable, but this early loss seems especially poignant, maybe because we were still getting to know him—and he was still getting to know himself. I realize there were so many adventures ahead. No one will ever know all that he might have been or done. But right now, on his birthday, it seems there is no dividing line—no gap between my spirit and his.

Day 112: The Gift of God's Understanding

I ONCE HEARD A STORY ABOUT A MINISTER DURING WORLD WAR II who was called to the home of a father who had lost his only son in battle. The father was distraught and yelled at the minister, "I want to know where God was when my only son was being killed!" The minister sat for a long time in silence, and then compassionately said, "I imagine God was in the same place He was when His Only Begotten Son was being killed."

This story reminds me of a conversation I had with my team captain after the graveside service. We had traveled out of state to have Brieson buried in my hometown. My captain, Julie, did not travel to this event, but she didn't forget about it. She texts me late that night asking how the service went. I reply that it had gone well. She then asks how I was doing. I respond, "I'm doing okay."

It's late, about 10 p.m., and I am lying in the dark in my oldest daughter's guest room, the light from my screen the only illumination in the room. I reread my last statement and then add, "I am not the first or only person to ever lose a son."

I meant this as a testament to the grief that so many others have experienced, and that even on that day of the service, my mother's next-door neighbor lost her son in a car accident. My aim is to convey to Julie that I know there are hundreds of thousands of people who have had this experience, and some in more difficult circumstances than mine have been.

But Julie did not take the meaning that way. Instead, she responded, "Yes, it makes it more obvious—the suffering of God."

It took me a few heartbeats to process that she meant the death of Jesus Christ, but when I grasped it, I felt as if she had walked right into my interior—that space we think is impenetrable but, when it's breeched, leaves us unable to speak. What a gift to have a friend who points me toward Jesus Christ and the eternal nature of things and not just the here and now.

Day 113: The Gift of Keeping Promises

My oldest son's wife, Christine, has started a blog of memories where everyone in our family can share experiences about Brieson. There are surprising stories listed—things I had never known during his life. As I'm reading through it today, I realize these are good memories to keep.

But what is possible to keep? Can I keep memories? Maybe a few, but most of them will fade away over time. It's hard to remember every moment of his life—well, impossible really. What is it that I'm trying to preserve? What do I really have the power to keep? I can keep going. I can keep my faith. I can keep an open mind. I can keep trying. I can keep looking forward.

But I can't keep people. They change. They evolve.

Brieson has already moved beyond the memories I have of him. Keeping memories of him appears to be some means of preserving his life, but that's not what is happening at all. I don't know how I know this. I can't point to any evidence in particular, but I just know that he's not the person in those stories or in those photos or in those memories anymore. He has grown beyond them. They are relics.

The most important things to keep are not the photos or the writings or the mementos but the promises. Those are the only things that really matter in the end. Everything else will be packed in a box and stored on a shelf. But promises are vibrant and affect his future.

I watched a documentary about a man who had lost his son during a suicide bombing. The father's life had basically stopped at that point.

His anger would not allow him to move on with his life. He kept in-
sisting that "nothing could replace his son—nothing!" In one way, he
was right, since nothing *could* replace his son. But in another way, he
was also wrong. To move on doesn't mean he's leaving his son behind;
it is not an act of disloyalty. Moving on is moving *toward* his son, who
has moved ahead of him and into his future. It is an act of integrity.

Promises are the structure for creating people of integrity. Honesty
is usually speaking words of truth *following* actions, but integrity consists of words of truth that *create* action. When a person of integrity makes a promise, one can rely on those words as future events.
Honesty is speaking truthfully about past reality; integrity is speaking
purposefully about future reality.

I don't feel that any promises have been broken. I guess others
might believe that God has let me down. After all, God promised me
something: that if I went to the temple, angels would watch over my
children. But I know that promise is still being fulfilled.[24] Nothing
has been tarnished, and nothing has been irrevocably lost.

In the early days of Brieson's death, people asked me what they
could do for me. I knew I didn't want compassion or pity. What I did
want was harder to determine. Today, I know what that something is:
keep your promises. Don't fail me in living what you believe. There
are few things more stabilizing for me than being in the presence of
someone who is trustworthy. Someone who follows through on even
the smallest promise, such as "I'll call you" or "Let's go to lunch," allows me to rest secure in the knowledge that there is something in my
life that will come to fruition. Conversely, there is nothing more wea-
rying than to be with a person who is handing me empty promises.

---

24. Elder Vaughn J. Featherstone of the Seventy once said, "I promise you that
all who faithfully attend to temple work will be blessed beyond measure.
Your families will draw closer to the Lord, unseen angels will watch over
your loved ones when satanic forces tempt them, the veil will be thin,
and great spiritual experiences will distill upon this people" ("I promise
you," AZ Quotes, accessed Aug. 17, 2023, https://www.azquotes.com/
quote/745109).

Day 123: The Gift of Not Rebelling

I am reading in the Book of Mormon this morning about Nephi leaving Jerusalem, and I suddenly see this story so differently. I realize how unhappy Nephi was to leave Jerusalem. All the wealth, opportunity, and future he had before him—who would be happy to leave all that behind? And all because your father said you should. I am sure Nephi wondered what the purpose was for all this. Why was their family being asked to do this? It all seemed so haphazard.

I have always identified with Laman and Lemuel and their disgruntled comments—their questioning of why this had to happen. Of course, this journey is ridiculous to them. They want the life they had envisioned—the life they had planned—and it was all behind them, all back in Jerusalem. They mourn the life they left behind. Therefore, they can never see the blessings and miracles happening all around them because they are always looking back at the widening chasm between what they wanted and what they were given.

I once understood this principle like seeing it on a postcard—accurate but safely within my grasp. Now I am standing on the lip of the Grand Canyon and both seeing and feeling the deepness, danger, and difficulty of this principle, knowing it is far beyond my control. The path ahead is not what I had planned, hoped for, or expected—especially when all my friends and relatives are still contentedly back in Jerusalem living the life I had wanted. I can see the chasm between us widening.

All this flashes across my mind as I come to this well-known verse. It's so simple that I have given it only a nodding recognition, but today it's in bold, flashing print: "Wherefore, I did cry unto the Lord" (1 Nephi 2:16).

The result? And maybe this is why I've breezed by it—because it once seemed like such a small answer: "And behold he did visit me, and did soften my heart that I did believe all the words which had been spoken by my father; wherefore, I did not rebel against him like unto my brothers" (1 Nephi 2:16).

Sometimes I wonder, What am I doing in this situation? How did I get here? I don't know. I guess most of the time I am simply going forth, like Nephi leaving Jerusalem. It sounds so thrilling in the scriptures, but the reality is extraordinarily more testing. Since I left the well-traveled path, it is remarkable how quickly my faith has come under question. It has even started to be labeled something else entirely—repression or foolishness perhaps.

And in the event I do put my faith in God, I still have many people on the same path murmuring and disapproving, continually telling me how God is misleading me.

I have a new respect for what a hard time this "chosen family" actually had. Faith sounds like an edifying way to travel, but sometimes I just want an airline ticket and a fixed itinerary.

Day 146: The Gift of Fringe

YEARS AGO WHILE TRAVELING TO UTAH, I WAS LISTENING TO A TALK by Elder Jeffrey R. Holland. About halfway through this talk, he said the following:

> I am convinced that one of the profound themes of the Book of Mormon is the role and prevalence and central participation of angels in the gospel story.
>
> One of the things that will become more important in our lives the longer we live is the reality of angels, their work and their ministry. I refer here not alone to the angel Moroni but also to those more personal ministering angels who are with us and around us, empowered to help us and who do exactly that (see 3 Ne. 7:18; Moro. 7:29–32, 37; D&C 107:20).[25]

I was immediately intrigued. *Angels? What angels?* This began a study of every tiny thing I could learn about angels.

I have a friend, Michele, who is just as enthralled by angels as I am. She also happens to do my lashes. I tell Michele some of my most personal stories. She serves as both a sounding board and an angelic

25. Jeffrey R. Holland, "For a Wise Purpose," *Ensign*, Jan. 1996, 16.

enabler. I always leave feeling my eyes have been opened in more ways than one.

I don't really need to get my lashes done, but I do need time with Michele. She is an unusual gift. Her common sense and life experiences widen the perspective of what I have lived and learned. Michele had a fiancé who took his own life, so she isn't hesitant to discuss suicide. That, along with our love of angels, gives us both a similar set of binoculars for seeing this world—and the next.

Michele begins adding a layer of fringe to my lashes. Of course she asks about me, and I am fully comfortable, both physically and spiritually, in sharing things I would struggle to explain to anyone else. She is open, generous, assuring, and kind.

Today we talk about angels again—now that I have the added experience of almost daily communications from the other side. She considers my recent experiences and adds more depth to my shallow reaching.

In studying the scriptures, which are filled with angelic encounters (in fact, there is hardly a story without one), these beings often enter and exit the story with hardly a blink, introduced so casually, like how one might mention a mailman in a story—just a well-known and ordinary part of everyone's life and a perfectly familiar way of delivering a message.

By this time, Michele and I have shared many stories, books, and all kinds of experiences about this topic. But now, after Brieson's death, the subject has taken an earnest turn, at least for me (perhaps it always was for her).

Before the eyelash appointment, I go back to some of the angel passages I have marked in the scriptures. Even though I have previously highlighted this story because of my own experiences, I now see something new: angels can wake us up (see Mosiah 3:2).

Angels come to tell us things—awaken our minds or consciousness to things around us. I have already experienced this dozens of times—practically daily. I realize that most of my heavenly communications come between 3 and 5 a.m. Is this a coincidence or a heavenly pattern? I am excited to discuss this with Michele.

During the appointment, we talk about it but eventually end up discussing angel wings. We both know angels don't have wings and that angels are often described that way to symbolize their power to move and act (see Doctrine and Covenants 77:4). Then this prophecy is brought back to my mind: He will arise "with healing in his wings" (Malachi 4:2; 3 Nephi 25:2; 2 Nephi 25:13).

Wings are a means of ascension, soaring, rising above, and giving broader perspective. The word *wings* comes from the Hebrew word *kanaph,* which can be translated as "wing, extremity, edge, hem, or fringe."[26]

Remember the woman who was healed by touching the fringe of Jesus' robe? She was testing the prophecy that the Messiah would come "with healing in his wings." She knew that if Jesus was the Messiah, she could be healed by merely touching the fringe of His robe. Her knowledge of this prophecy, followed by her actions of faith in the prophecy, healed her (see Mark 5:25–34).

As Michele is talking, all this unifies into a new awareness. Mourning is a time of decline, descent, reduction, and narrowing of focus. God doesn't promise He will keep us from injury. Instead, He says that in the midst of our bruises, afflictions, and sorrows, He will pick us up and carry us to higher understanding. *This* is the healing in His wings.

How can one small item of truth be so restorative? I feel like a paper napkin touching water, drawing liquid into myself. In much the same way, I imagine that the woman, thirsty for God's cure, absorbed healing after touching the hem of His robe. All these ideas settle into me like a substance entering each molecule, not only soaking up the pain but refreshing me as well.

---

26. The King James Version translates *kanaph* as *wing* 74 times, *borders* 2 times, *corners* 2 times, *ends* 2 times, *feathers* 2 times, *sort* 2 times, *winged* 2 times, and miscellaneous words 8 times. (See "Strong's H3671," Blue Letter Bible, accessed Aug. 17, 2023, https://www.blueletterbible.org/lexicon/h3671/kjv/wlc/0-1/.)

Day 149: The Gift of Contemplation

WHEN OPPRESSIVE MEMORIES AND NAGGING FEARS AND ANXIETIES of lost opportunities begin to encroach on me, I do what I always do: start writing. There is something about getting things out of my head and onto paper (like I'm doing right now) that is healing for me. Somehow exposing these concerns to light makes them seem less turbulent, as if now I control them. Getting ink onto paper is a step in discovering and then managing.

As I write, things often come out in short phrases or lists. These are sometimes crayon scrawls of spiritual expression, but later they become instruments of illumination and discernment. They help me hunt down the scrambling rats in my cellar, trap them, label them, and hang them as specimens for further study.

I have several lists that have helped me, and I add to them occasionally, but usually they are finished in one setting because I need to get them out at that moment. These lists include the following:

- Things I Love about Brieson
- Things I Miss about Brieson
- How Does God Feel about Me?
- Things I Have Never Asked For but Were Given to Me Anyway
- People Who Remembered on the Two-Year Anniversary
- Morning Routines That Benefit Me Emotionally
- What Resiliency Looks Like
- Doctrines That Sustain Me
- What Brings Me Energy / What Drains My Energy
- Miracles and Tender Mercies I Have Experienced
- Practices That Help Me Feel Peace

Compiling these lists brings something illusive into a kind of concreteness. All of these things that are happening to me are imperceptible to others, even though each of these lists has the names of many individuals cataloged within them.

Sometimes it's difficult to stand between these two worlds: one in which the very atmosphere seems to be nourishing me, and one in which others sincerely believe is a godless world. Despite how it may appear, we all have a fear of jumping to the wrong conclusions. Nearly all new experiences are frightening and bring feelings of hesitation and resistance—a kind of leaning away from the moment, which diminishes leaping range.

Today it comes to me that from what I have read about God, He doesn't often offer seat belts or other safety features to even His most valiant disciples. Yet these same faith-filled leapers always return eager to tell us how incredible their experiences have been.

Actuary charts do little to mitigate our fears, although they are based on sound science. Instead, actual hearts stirring in response to spiritual assurances allow us to take those leaps of faith.

Day 151: The Eclipse

THE LARGEST SOLAR ECLIPSE IN ALMOST A HUNDRED YEARS IS SCHEDuled for today. Brieson had been long looking forward to this event. The media calls it "the Great American Eclipse" because it will be a total solar eclipse visible inside a band that spans the entire United States, from the Pacific to Atlantic coasts.

Before he died, Brieson created a Google Invite to remind us of this event. A few days before the eclipse, I receive the invite right on time: *Brieson has invited you to this event. Are you attending?* That was both a chilling and heartening invitation: a message *from* heaven pointing *to* heaven.

My daughter-in-law, Christine, a fourth-grade teacher, knew how much this event meant to Brieson and began a project for her entire school months in advance. When the local news media learned of her efforts, she was interviewed by numerous radio, magazine, and TV stations. Eventually, places as far as England were calling and asking to talk with her. She did all of this to honor Brieson, although she did not advertise it that way. All of us in the family knew it, especially me.

Today—Monday, August 21, 2017—Courtney, Siearra, and I gather at Christine's school to watch the eclipse. It's an overcast day (an unusual circumstance in Arizona) with hazy, fluffy, and muddy clouds floating overhead. All morning my emotions are twanging and strumming, one moment melodious and congruent, the next jarring and discordant. I have expectations for this day, but I fear getting them too high and anticipating too much.

We park and walk to Christine's classroom, then as a group (like all elementary school events) we march out to our specific spot on the field. The clouds continue to obscure the eclipse. We wait out on the grass for something to open up behind the clouds.

Christine comments that this is something Brieson would love: instead of just watching the eclipse, now we have to wait for these dramatic glimpses. At each brief sighting, all the kids rush to put on their glasses and gaze upward, and simultaneously there is a gush of "oohs" and "aahs" across the field, for just a minute or so, until another cloud shifts and the eclipse is lost to our view. Then the kids go back to chasing each other across the field or congregating in tight little knots of exclusion.

I sit on the grass listening to the laughter and the yelling. No one is talking to me, no one is sitting beside me, and despite the large group of kids, I feel a great amount of personal space. I slide on my darkened glasses and gaze upward at the thick bank of clouds. Occasionally, a few rays of light leak through, streaming like honey.

There is a kind of tension in the watching and waiting—a hoping, a looking forward to, laced with impatience. I am wondering if Brieson is here as well; surely he would not miss this event. But I don't feel him here.

Soon the clouds shift again and the eclipse slides into view. I watch as the moon edges across it, the sun becoming less visible and, at one point, not visible at all. Effectively, that was what I had come to see: a celestial body becoming invisible to me.

Although the orb is gone, I can see the gossamer corona and know it for what it is—my sun. It doesn't look or act like the sun I have seen all my life, but with no instruction at all, I know it is still there and still functioning just as it always has. The moon that acts as a veil between us does not throw doubt onto my former knowledge and experience.

I get that feeling of smallness and insignificance in relation to the vastness of the universe. I am stretching thinner and thinner. My heartstrings are twanging and strumming, discordant and jarring. Then suddenly, quite abruptly, all the strings inside me still at once—and there's complete peace. It's as if someone has very gently and deliberately reached down and laid a finger across the frets.

In that moment, there is no one I would rather be than me.

Day 167: The Gift of Being Trusted

TOMORROW I AM LEAVING ON A SIXTEEN-DAY VACATION TO ENGLAND. This is a trip we've been planning since January, months before Brieson's death. As I'm making lists, checking items, printing out tickets, and packing my suitcase, my cell phone rings. It's Gayla, a former ward member.

Gayla is not someone who calls me very often—maybe once every five years or so. Curious, I answer. She chats for a moment and then asks if I would be interested in doing a newsletter for the Arizona Phoenix Mission.

Ummm. I hesitate. "Are you sure? I don't know anything about graphic design or sending out mass emails." I can't imagine how my name would have come up for this or why I would be thought of since this is not in my talent wheelhouse.

She assures me that independently, both she and her husband thought of me for this assignment. I'm surprised because I can easily think of several people who would be more qualified, but since I've been asking for something to do for over a year, I accept. Beggars can't be choosers.

Later Scott, Gayla's husband, calls to confirm my response and give me more details. I rush to let him know that I have no idea how to do this and that I'm leaving the country for sixteen days tomorrow. He tells me that the September newsletter is complete and that I'll be starting with the October edition.

After I hang up and the nervousness settles a little, I realize what a gift Scott and Gayla have just extended to me: confidence and trust.

They are both fully aware that this is not something I have ever done, but it is almost as if they are saying, "I know Shelly, and she will figure it out." What a vote of confidence! And in that moment, a feeling of being trusted returns to me, without me even realizing that I had lost that somewhere along the road. With this assignment comes the subtle message, "You are competent. You are capable. We trust you."

After returning from England, I start looking for formats, templates, and color schemes. President Collins asks me to send him a mock-up. I do. He is generous with his praise. After completing the first edition, we happen to be at his home for a "Shake and Bake," a fun get-together where he'd make milkshakes and we'd bring baked goods. He seeks me out and again applauds this first edition, later telling me that he has shared it with other mission presidents as well.

Perhaps to him this is a small thing—something he does with everyone—but to me, at this time in my life, it is feels like winning a Pulitzer. I have felt left out, set on a shelf, discarded, and untrusted. I cannot remember the last time a leader praised anything I did. I had forgotten what it felt like to have someone actually pleased with my efforts and encouraging of my ideas.

Scott and Gayla have given me a platform for healing—a kind of therapeutic remedy. Re-creation is part of every act of healing, and I will be creating every month in a small way. This project fully pulled my attention and efforts and helped me feel like I could look more deeply instead of looking away.

Day 181: The Gift of the Best Things

I AM STILL IN ENGLAND WITH ASHLEY, KRISTA, AND KATE, MY BOOK club friends. This trip has been a needed break from my routine. Later I read that travel is one of the best ways to assuage grief, but for now, I'm just enjoying all their company and the new things I am seeing and learning. This is not just a change of location; it is also a reprieve from grieving. It's a time away from confronting the same situations, ideas, and feelings.

As part of our trip, Ashley wants to shop at Harrods of London, the world's largest luxury department store. I don't like to shop, especially at a place where I can't afford anything, but I go along interested to witness what they are trying to describe to me.

It's an impressive store, with incredible and unique items everywhere I turn. From the first moment, it's apparent that this is a store for the wealthiest of customers. Ashley is right: it's an adventure to see the exotic items, the deferential clerks, and the outrageous price tags.

Browsing through a gift nook, I run across a small box labeled "Best Things." Curious, I open it. Inside are small cards, each printed with something free that can bring happiness. I riffle through them and am struck by the idea:

- Waking up to the sun shining
- The people who never gave up on me
- The feeling of hope
- Trying something new for the first time
- YouTube cat videos
- Someone to hold your hand
- Inside jokes
- Finding something you've been actively looking for

I carry the box around for about thirty minutes, contemplating whether to pay the exorbitant price. I am cognizant of the irony of finding a box listing common, ordinary gifts from God in what must be one of the world's most materialistic places.

Eventually I put it back on the table and decide to make my own list.

This little idea became invaluable to me. The underlying purpose is to recognize the seemingly common, ordinary things that spark a feeling of joy mingled with contentment. The list would, of course, be unique to each person. That's the point—pay attention to your own feelings and note what elevates and comforts you. I was surprised how easily my list grew:

- Falling asleep by the pool
- Someone who laughs when I laugh

- Learning something brand new that changes my viewpoint or expands my understanding
- Libraries
- Poetry
- Being alone outside at night
- Crossing something off my to-do list
- Conversing with a person who is passionate about the same things I care about, who can easily pick up the thread even when I speak in half-formed sentences
- Watching someone's face relax with relief because they got the answer or understanding they needed
- Getting a text from a friend
- Finding the exact word I'm looking for

There's more—a lot more—but this gives a taste of what the list entails. I was humbly surprised at how many gifts God always has on hand for me—for everyone really. It's like a cookie jar of satisfying pleasures.

Great things are not needed to feel happiness. Size and length are not necessary to experience the magnitude of God. A microsecond can have eternal scope.

Day 189: The Gift of Healing Forests

I RESERVE BOOKS AT THE PUBLIC LIBRARY QUITE OFTEN. TODAY AN email arrives saying a book is waiting for me at the Agave Branch. When I get to the library and pull it from the holds shelf, I am a little taken aback. The book is titled *The Hidden Life of Trees.*[27]

Hmmm. I don't remember requesting this book. I skim the jacket blurb. It's a nonfiction, scientific book written by a forest ranger in Germany about—you guessed it—trees. I still have no recollection

---

27. Peter Wohlleben, *The Hidden Life of Trees: What They Feel, How They Communicate—Discoveries from a Secret World* (London: Allen Lane, 2016).

of this book or why I would have been interested in it. I must have requested it a long time ago.

I still check it out and take it home. As I begin to read, I'm profoundly struck by the author's explanation of trees' existence that parallels my own experience. He explains that scientists have discovered that trees actually help each other. In the past, the ruling premise had been that in order to have the best timber production, the trees needed to be thinned so they'd have more room to grow. But now they've discovered that trees form a network that actually strengthens each individual tree. The entire assertion of the book is simply this: forests make good timber.

That may seem obvious at first glance, but it's actually quite profound. For instance, the trees' branches grow out just enough to lightly touch the branches of the neighboring trees, and then they stop. This allows each tree to get the maximum amount of sunlight, and it also encourages the tree trunks to grow straight up. The close proximity of the trees creates a climate conducive to keeping the ground cool, thus retaining needed moisture. The trees actually work together despite the appearance that they are in competition for sunlight and moisture.

This grouping also protects the trees from strong winds and shelters them from the harshness of the elements. And, most surprisingly, scientists find that when an individual tree receives a shock—such as a disease or a nick in its trunk or even an infestation—the other trees will send nourishment to the injured tree's roots, sometimes from miles away. Even after the tree has been cut down, the neighboring trees will continue to send sugar for months and months to its roots in hopes of reviving the stump.

This is an incredible analogy for the experience I've been having. It negates the assertion that a tree growing on the side of the cliff is more to be admired than the one growing in the midst of the forest. This cliff-hanging tree is often used as an illustration of faith or tenacity as it sends its roots deep into solid rock. I am not disputing that the tree on the side of the cliff *will* survive, but its trunk will be twisted and its branches gnarled. It will not produce good timber, good shade, or good fruit. Only forests or orchards can produce those things.

I recognize anew the incredible gift I have been given of miles and miles of thick forest that surround me. I receive sugar daily, sometimes from a great distance. The proximity of others has protected and sheltered me, and many stalwart examples have kept me vertical while sharing the light. I have been planted in the midst of an incredible forest.

I know some people say that they are spiritual but don't believe in organized religion. But the way I see it, that's like saying I love flying but don't believe in airports. Without that system and structure, you can only get so far. I can't imagine going through this without the huge ward forest that surrounds me.

In this moment I realize that I have known for years that this Church teaches truth—for decades, in fact. But only now am I beginning to realize the power of having a community of Saints—being part of a group that promotes my vertical growth, softens the winds of adversity, and even sends me healing sugars from miles away for years. This is truly an organizational ecosystem of healing.

Part of grief is losing someone and then realizing after they're gone all that their absence entails. But this is just the opposite. I have discovered something that has always been there—I just never saw it. I wonder if God ever gets exasperated with my relentless obtuseness.[28]

Day 241: The Gift of the Imperfect

CHURCH HAS JUST ENDED FOR THE DAY, AND I AM WALKING ACROSS the parking lot toward my car. I see Thomas coming toward me, a man I know from the ward. I assume we will pass with a nod or a smile. Instead, he stops, his small son in tow.

Thomas says, "I just wanted to tell you that I'm sorry about your son."

---

28. Later I find this verse: "To appoint unto them that mourn in Zion, to give unto them beauty for ashes, the oil of joy for mourning, the garment of praise for the spirit of heaviness; that they might be called trees of righteousness, the planting of the Lord, that he might be glorified" (Isaiah 61:3)

Thomas never met my son—never knew him. I would not have expected, in the furthest reaches of my mind, for him to speak to me of it—especially now, over six months later. His son tugs at his suit coat, leaning out away from him.

I smile and thank him. There is a short silence and I start to move away. But he continues.

"When my brother died, I said I will always acknowledge others' losses, but I haven't. And I just want to say what I haven't said: how very sorry I am—that we all are—to hear of your loss. It has been hard for you, I know." He chokes up and swallows it down.

My glass blooms into light.

He could have waited for the perfect time or the perfect place or the perfect words. Instead, he just went ahead and did it, right there when the opportunity presented itself—right there in the parking lot with his son tugging away at his suit. There's nothing astounding in his speech or unusual about his feelings, but the moment crystallizes in my mind. I try to smile, but there is too fierce a feeling welling up inside me.

Sometimes the perfect becomes the enemy of the good. As I walk away, I realize something about myself: I am constantly waiting for that lined-up opportunity, and that has always been my downfall. I have good intentions, but I am held up by the timing or the environment or the mood. I need to learn from Thomas and stop waiting for that ideal moment and instead take the opportunity and let the Spirit perfect it.

I guess that's why I could not bring myself to visit Pam when Ryan died. I was all pretense and presumption. I wanted to do it perfectly, and since no one is perfect, I couldn't do it at all. Now, after months of people stumbling over words and offering awkward condolences to me, I can tell you this for certain: it is better to do something imperfectly than to do nothing flawlessly.

As I walk away, I think, "I will never be reluctant again to help someone in grief." Turns out that isn't an easy promise to keep.

Day 218: The Gift of Deflection

I HAVE A TENNIS MATCH AT THE WIGWAM RESORT THIS EVENING IN the city of Goodyear. On the way there, something comes on the radio that pushes a drizzling cloud into my throat. I struggle to get myself under control and even-keeled again. *Why am I even going to this match? I should turn around and go home right now.* But I don't. I keep driving, palming tears from my face and squeezing emotions back into place.

When I get to the Wigwam, I warm up, not feeling especially like engaging with anyone or really even wanting to play. I have almost no energy or desire to compete. Then Steve, my partner, shows up and we are sent to our court.

We get down 0–4 right from the start, mostly because Steve hasn't warmed up. Then everything turns around and we end up winning 6–4. The same thing happens in the second set. Through the entire match, Steve is buoyant and encouraging—just so much pure, ridiculous, spontaneous fun that all my inward systems are moved from standby red-alert to unblinking green.

When we're done, because we're the last team to finish, everyone is standing by our court. We walk outside the fence and wiggle into the group—it's a big circle of people now. Everyone is joking and laughing. The sun has set, and long shadows are falling across the grass behind us. I am fine—more than fine. I'm having a good time. Something is said and I laugh.

Suddenly, very clearly into my mind comes an accusing voice: *Why are you laughing? You shouldn't be laughing.* I am brought up sharp. This has never happened before. What is this? Everyone continues in the same atmosphere of lighthearted fun. Meanwhile, I am tipping backward, past the point of balance, grappling.

Allan, one of the team captains, is on the far side of the circle from me. Instantaneously, he takes three steps across the circle and hugs me, whispering in my ear, "I have never acknowledged your son's death, and I just want you to know that I'm sorry."

This is so sudden and out of tune with the rest of what's going on that everyone stops talking and looks at us. I nod at Allan, not answering because I am stunned. It is as if he had seen the gloom spiraling toward me and quickly stepped between me and darkness, deflecting it away.

To everyone else, it appeared that Allan just leapt across the circle and hugged me for no reason at all. There is a moment of perplexed silence as everyone stares at us. Then, when neither of us explains, they pick the conversation back up and get back to laughing.

Perhaps Allan thought his condolences were offered too late or in less-than-ideal circumstances, but it was actually perfectly timed and fully responsive to the state I was in, telling me that only God could have inspired it. And honestly, it was from the most unlikely person imaginable. Now I know why people are shocked when angels arrive—because they aren't at all what you expect.

Day 220: The Gift of a Loving Parent

THE TAKING OF A LIFE IS A SERIOUS THING, NOT A MATTER THAT CAN be lightly brushed over. I have thought on this for many hours. I do not know the criteria or the answers.

However, as I am reading today about Alma's experience with eternal torment, I see something new. As Alma was "racked . . . with the pains of a damned soul" and "harrowed up by the memory of [his] many sins" (Alma 36:16–17), he remembered what his father had said about "the coming of one Jesus Christ" (Alma 36:17).

Now here is one thing I *do* know—because I saw it.

One night, Brieson was upset about God—about religion. He was telling my husband and me about why he didn't believe in God and saw religion as a farce. My husband listened, paused, and then with a great calmness said, "Brieson, I want your happiness. It is all I've ever wanted for my children. I am telling you that this is the way to ever-lasting happiness. I would never lie to you."

Brieson glared at us for a long moment, and then I saw something shift inside him. A tangible peace descended across the room; it felt like something I was wearing instead of feeling. I saw some hardness in Brieson soften, so much so that he seemed to collapse in on himself. He made no retort. There was more silence, but it wasn't the silence of absence or defense—it was a silence of presence and acceptance.

If the sealing power binds us to our parents and our children, and this is the greatest power from God that we have access to on this earth, then I wonder how this works. If it's possible for a parent to go into hell and retrieve a child, then there is no question my husband would do it. And if someone's life must be forfeited to appease justice, then there will be no doubt whose life will be given. Anyone who knows my husband will accept this without hesitation.

And yet as good and as full of integrity as my husband is, he is not God. God's nature dwarfs his nature infinitely. This knowledge constricts the circumference of my grief. I do not worry about whether God is working to get Brieson out of hell, if indeed he ever went there. I know that God is a superior Father, a skilled and omniscient Father. Why would I doubt His character now? I do not worry that God is penalizing Brieson unnecessarily, like some sort of dungeon experience. It defies all I know of God.

He is a just God, certainly. But when mercy is in order, He runs to offer it. God's work is to bring about the immortality and eternal life of man (see Moses 1:39), and He is the Master at His craft.

Day 231: The Gift of Nature

THE WEATHER IS COOLING DOWN, AND I TAKE SEVERAL WALKS EACH week and just allow nature to minister to me. Nature has a deep soothing and restful quality. My usual artificial world of Facebook, Instagram, texting, and Netflix never leaves me with the same feeling of connection that five minutes in nature does.

Although it will be a long time until I see Brieson again, I now perceive God's nurture in this delay instead of His indifference. "Wait upon the Lord" is an instruction and gift being offered to me. Impatience has a way of bypassing nurturing. Maybe this is what people are referring to when they say "quality time." Quality time is nurturing time—a very careful and attentive encouragement of growth.

I now realize how patient God has been with me all my life. President Dieter F. Uchtdorf once said, "*Love* is really spelled *t-i-m-e*."[29] Even though I forget almost everything from general conference a few weeks out, I have never forgotten this phrase. It comes back to me powerfully today, and in a split-second, multiple connections are formed.

When we devote time to someone, it indicates their worth to us. Time is a precious commodity in this world. When I spend or invest that precious commodity on someone, I raise their worth.

Development is a process of time. Planting, weeding, watering, pruning—it all costs time. A grieving person is always a waiting person—looking at a patch of ground, full of belief that something hidden beneath the surface will manifest itself in the future.

Waiting on the Lord is anything but passive, however. It's not just something I should engage in half-heartedly. Rather, my waiting should be marked with expectation instead of frustration, weeding instead of needing, patience instead of defense.

All these realizations and reassurances come because I have left my synthetic life to go out into wildlife. And I am struck anew at the strangeness of this experience. Grief is like picking up all your thoughts, attitudes, and beliefs and moving them into a whole new dimension overnight. I wonder about things I have never wondered about. I see myself and my place in this world quite differently now. This experience is not easy, nor comfortable, but it isn't always painful either. Some of it is pure awe.

Day 232: The Gift of Exculpation

I ATTEND IRAN'S SONS' FUNERALS TODAY. (IRAN AND I BOTH PLAY AT the same tennis facility.) He lost two sons in the same day in a traffic

---

29. Dieter F. Uchtdorf, "Of Things That Matter Most," *Ensign* or *Liahona*, Nov. 2010, 21.

accident—a tragic event, and like all unexpected and early deaths, heartrending and confusing.

I meet my friend Lynette at the church and we go in to find a seat. We are early and therefore get to see everyone else arriving. This is not my first funeral since Brieson's death, but it's the first of someone with a son who has died. I don't know Iran extremely well, yet I know that this event will move him right into the world I occupy, and I want to make sure—wish I could ensure—that the transition is supported and guided.

I think some people are surprised to see me here, as if a funeral would be the most unlikely place to find a bereaved person. The truth is, I am no longer afraid of death. I haven't been for a very long time since studying near-death experiences. I know this world tells you that this life is all that there is and that we should cling to it with a tenacity bordering on terrified panic. I know this life is necessary, but it is not the culmination of who you are or who you will become.

I see the hesitation, the discomfort, and the heavy sorrow as everyone enters the sanctuary. Death is so familiar to me now that I can look on it kindly, though I know that others still see it as something to be ashamed of, like perhaps they should have stopped it. This is a common, human response. We take too much credit for our ability to sustain life.

On Monday, I was working on the Crisis Response van—a second responder unit that helps with on-scene crises—and we were called to a death in Goodyear. The widow had taken her husband to the doctor five days previously and been told that he was in a precarious state of health, unlikely to last through the month. Five days later he passed away watching TV in his lounge chair. It was a peaceful death, easily seen from his face and his positioning.

Still, she blames herself: "I should have checked on him." This couple lived in a thousand-square-foot house. She was within eyesight of him practically every moment, and his passing was so easy that she didn't realize it had happened. Yet she's distraught. "I lost him. I lost him," she keeps repeating—as if she's been careless, or if only she had done the right thing at the right time, he would still be with her. I could sympathize with her shock, but I wanted to assure her that this is not her fault.

After attending numerous deaths on the Crisis Response van, I can tell you that no matter the circumstances of the death, there is a highly remote, almost non-existent possibility that some action would have prevented the death. We can only do what we know in the moment. Death is inevitable—we all die. I don't think God is surprised by anyone's entrance into heaven. I wonder, over and over, why we take so much responsibility for death. Almost every person I encountered on the Crisis Response van felt that the passing of the deceased was somehow preventable. No matter the age, no matter the health, no matter the circumstances, they felt like they should have stopped it.

Thinking this way seems unfruitful. It only adds pain to the grief if I take on a responsibility that was not mine. I think that in the end, this blocks necessary acceptance. My greatest fear is that Iran will take this on himself. I wish I could tell him all I know, all I understand, and all I have experienced, but grieving is so much a matter of choice. I hope he chooses acceptance, not resistance.

Day 247: The Gift of Timely Support

I'M SITTING AT MY DAUGHTER'S HOUSE IN UTAH. IT'S THE DAY AFTER Thanksgiving, and I am working on the mission newsletter. I hear a ding on my phone and look over to see a message from Trudi:

"I lost Cameron this morning. Passed away."

What?! In that moment I feel as if I have been stripped of every ounce of color I possess. *I just had lunch with Trudi last week, and we talked about Cameron and her worries for him. And now he's gone? How old is he? Seventeen? What has happened?* All the usual questions and concerns course through my mind, and I am right back to March 23rd, my feelings tipping out all over the place.

I try calling, but she isn't answering her phone. I am frantically dialing and texting anyone in Arizona who might know something. No one knows anything. It looks like I am first to hear—and I am six hundred miles away. I have that despairing helpless feeling coming over me. I text back:

"Oh Trudi I am so sorry. I know the tragedy of this moment. Let people love you, Trudi. So many people will want to help you. I know how hard it is to be open when it hurts so much and you just want to be alone and process it. But let people come, Trudi. It helps the healing. I promise."

Suddenly, my phone dings with a new text, this one from an unknown number. It says, "Been thinking of you. Just want to say thank you for being one of the few to make us feel so welcome in the ward when we first moved here."

Since this contact is not in my phone, I look up the number on my ward roster. It's a woman named Savannah. *What in the world?* I might have talked to her once or twice maybe. How implausible it is that she would text me now, eight months later, at this exact moment of need? She hardly knows me and certainly doesn't know Trudi. She would have no awareness of what is coursing through me at this moment. My scribbling feelings are paused—the pen is lifted.

As I'm reading Savannah's text and looking up her number, a new text arrives. This one is also from an unknown number, but the sender identifies himself:

"Hi Shelly. It's Justin. Hey, I ran into Billye Anne at the store this morning. She told me that your son had passed away. I am so sorry. I don't have a FB page or anything so I didn't know. My heart is breaking for you and your family. Let me extend my deepest sympathies to you all. I'm sure he is and ever will be an amazing son. Take hope in the plan of salvation. My sincere prayers are with you. Take care, my friend. Hope to see you sometime soon."

Everything inside me erases—a pure blank slate. I pause because I can't decide what conclusion to draw. I can't even remember the last time I saw Justin. Was it fifteen years ago? I don't know. Slowly a sketch begins to form on my slate—a faint penciling. I can't take my attention from it, and my glass is spraying prisms.

I answer Justin with a simple thank you, not knowing how to let him know that the timing of his text made it loaded with weight and power. I can hardly take in that (1) he got my number, (2) he actually acted on the prompting to text me, (3) he sent the text at the most auspicious moment, and (4) his words are a salve to the very things I am feeling in that moment.

Justin responds, "You take care of yourself. You've always been a great example and a great friend to me whether you knew it or not."

And just like that, the sketch has become a full-color animation and a vivid feeling washes over me. I can hardly compute the unlikeliness of two such random people texting me at the exact moment when I needed to pull my emotions back toward God. The odds are staggering.

Day 249: Inside the Fence

WE DRIVE BACK FROM UTAH TODAY, QUICKLY CHANGE OUR CLOTHES, and head to Trudi's house. We are greeted at the door by her mother who informs us that she is resting in the bedroom. I say, "Okay. Please let her know that Shelly and Stacey came by to see her."

"Wait," she says. "Trudi has been wanting to talk to you. I will get her up." A few minutes later Trudi comes out of the room. As soon as I see her, all my feelings of loss double in a moment.

I know she is expecting some kind of wisdom from me, as if I have been to the dead-end canyon and know some kind of secret passage out.

We sit down on the couch. My husband goes out to talk with Wes, Trudi's husband. Trudi is caved in. I put my hand on her arm and say, "It's going to be all right, but not for the reasons you think. I hope you will believe me when I say that you need to forget what you might have read about grief and about life and death. This is much different than you think it will be. There will be gifts—many, many gifts."

It is so hard to restrain myself. Trudi and I have shared so many spiritual stories and insights with each other over the years. I want to just pour it all out. I want her to know that these gifts will come in ways that she has never imagined nor can possibly describe. They are effervescent, ephemeral things that will lift her straight into God's encircling arms. I want her to know she will have different expectations now—not better or worse than anyone else's, just different. And mourning is all about reordering those expectations. Don't hang on to the usual, common ones. This new path will bring many moments of joy—it isn't a penalizing path.

She nods at me, but I can see it is all too soon. So I stop. I know she will remember none of this. The first week is just a blur. I can see she is still in the grip of the first terrors, with the idea that this was somehow her fault. We sit in silence for a few moments. My heart leaps at her, but she doesn't catch it and it falls between us.

I see that I need to give her time and respect her private processing. There is no reason for me to push my way into her tender and personal emotions. I know the necessity of staking out space and time to grapple with this. I don't want to divide her faith or force a confidence, and yet I have never so much wanted to be inside someone's fence before.

Day 250: Bearing It

OF COURSE, I AM THINKING ABOUT TRUDI AND SUZANNE TODAY AND wondering how they slept last night—what their concerns are and what they're reframing. Suzanne, who I know from church, lost a daughter a few days after Trudi lost her son. Each has a different scenario, but the end result is the same: their child is gone. I know how straining this initial effort is. It's like a constant battle of wills—the desire to submit and the desire to cave in. They seem the same but they're worlds apart.

Many people have been texting and calling me about Trudi and Suzanne. There is a definite expectation here that I will know what to do and what to say to bring some kind of comfort to them. I realize this same thing must have happened to Pam when my son died. But the problem is, although I have learned legions of things, I am not sure how to give it to others. Is grief completely unique, or are there universal elements to this process?

I feel incomprehensibly weary after these months of holding up, and this added grief of Trudi, Iran, and Suzanne quite suddenly becomes almost unbearable. Even though I usually carry my grief with resignation and determination, both those characteristics seem wholly inadequate with this added sorrow. The laws of physics say that when there is added strain and pressure, then there has to be additional support or else something is going to break.

This could be it. This might be the point where I cannot hold up with all the people who are counting on me to help them too.

Suddenly, sharply, and vividly, a scene from a movie comes into my mind. I don't know the title, the actors, or the plot, yet with distinct clarity, my mind plays out the following interaction.

A man and a woman are in a kitchen. The woman is weeping—uncontrollably sobbing. She cries, "It's too hard! I can't bear it. It's too much."

The man is angry—incredibly angry. He slams down his palm, hard and flat, onto the table next to her and yells, "Never say that! Never! You have no idea how much you can bear. No idea at all."

These words echo again and again through my mind: "You have no idea how much you can bear. No idea at all."

I think about the Holocaust victims and the hundreds of stories I have read about these sufferers—their difficult circumstances, their fears, their pains. Yet I only know these stories because they survived to tell them. They had things happen to them that seemed inconceivable to survive, and yet they picked their lives up and went right on living.

In many ways I have not really been invested in this world like I used to be. Of course, I have gone about my daily tasks in a kind of misty way. I don't reach out to people. I don't plan much. I don't care much about winning or losing. All the things of this world seem like so much dust to me now. They're just things I did to get from one moment to the next—not really things I did for any reason but more for the sake of action. Trudi's and Suzanne's losses have now awakened me to possible purpose.

In this moment, however, I feel like such a failure—so unprepared and self-centered. And I blame myself for not being able to help Trudi and Suzanne. I should have realized one purpose to all this is surely to help someone else along the path. In this moment I wish I were someone else—someone better.

Day 274: The Gift of Harboring

FOR THE PAST FEW DAYS I HAVE NOT BEEN FEELING THE SAME. I SEEM to have fallen from enchantment. I am gasping and flailing as if I have been treading water, always imagining myself capable of standing at any time, but then when I finally reach down to find the bottom, there is only liquid and I realize I am out of my depth. The testing period seems to have become more earnest.

I wake up feeling forsaken and I let that feeling fester (mistake number one). I open up Facebook (mistake number two). As I scroll through the feed, I see all the kindness being offered to others, and a kind of resentment builds up inside of me. These posts have never affected me before, but today they seem to bring an ache of stifled desires, the sharp pain of neglected needs, and something tapping away at my bruised and tender feelings.

I make a decision that even in this moment *I* know is petty, but I rationalize it away—I deserve this! Rashly, I text my daughter Carissa, asking her to post something on my Facebook page. She is reluctant but also senses that something deeper is at play. In a few moments, a post appears on my page.

The post reads, "You are so quiet; I forget you are suffering."

The post sits there with no likes or comments for over two hours. It is then that I notice it has been posted privately, not publicly, and I feel a gush of embarrassment mingled with gratitude for my daughter. Immediately, I recognize that her actions have provided a protected harbor for me—a space for me to restock and redirect. This realization is followed by a deep sense of the Spirit's disappointment with me.[30]

My glass flashes, its reflective quality inviting me to check myself—analyze and inspect.

Why did I do this? What is my motive here? What am I trying to gain? God is already giving me more on a daily basis than I could ever plan or detail on my own. Why did I feel a need to do this?

I see that I have downgraded myself by turning from God to social media. Others have always been sent—I don't need to be calling them up. They all come with omniscient preciseness and particularity in exactly the manner needed.

I realize that by being reactive, I have mixed it up: although grief is a time of self-absorption, it is not a time of selfishness. No one is entitled to be selfish. I have known for a long time that humility is the foundation of all spiritual growth, and now I am ashamed of—even mortified at—my selfish attempt at attention.

I was trying to elevate my suffering to something greater—trying to believe that my sorrow transcends ordinary misery and that it's somehow beyond my endurance. But the reality is, it's death—which couldn't be more common. It happens every day—actually, every second of every day. It is the familiar and known end to all our stories. I have no claim to the extraordinary.

I quickly hide the post from my timeline, despite the fact that no one but Carissa, God, and I could ever see it. Lesson learned. Although I can't feel God with me at this exact moment, I know He is on His way. There are better things ahead if I just keep my promise.

Still, sometimes as I wait, I can't help feeling like a Russian nesting doll—just sitting on the shelf hoping for someone to twist off the top and see what's inside: a smaller me, a more concentrated me, a

---

30. Many years later, I attend a fifth Sunday lesson taught by Jill Anderson who suggested that before posting on social media, consider whether you are serving your offering on a pedestal or a platter. A platter is meant for food to be passed around and shared, for nourishment and social exchange. A pedestal, on the other hand, is meant to display, to worship, to admire. Sometimes we don't even want to eat the food on a pedestal because it seems like eating it will ruin it. This seems like exactly the opposite of what serving should be.

more purified me, a more valuable me. Everything I need to face this tragedy is already inside of me, and layers of fluff are simply being tossed aside.

I realize all of this, but at the same time, sometimes it's just so hard to reduce yourself.

Day 298: The Gift of "I Pledge"

I DRIVE DOWNTOWN FOR AN ORIENTATION WITH A NEW VOLUNTEER group that I'm training to join. This organization, unbeknownst to me when I applied, is founded by a woman whose son committed suicide. When the director is explaining the history of the organization to me over the phone, she mentions that it all began because this young man had taken his life. I tell her that I have had a similar experience. She is immediately compassionate and suggests I meet with the founder.

So here I am today with this mother in her living room. She begins by asking me about my experience with suicide. I sketch the story very briefly. She asks no further questions. Instead, she almost interrupts me to tell her own experience. This is not necessarily a new situation for me; in fact, it's a common human tendency. If I tell my story, the other person usually relates their story as well. Sometimes it invites sharing and mutual understanding, but in this case, her story and her experience are colored by so much denial that I cannot enter into her feelings. I sit somewhat uncomfortably as tears of resentment well up in her eyes and then I watch as anger overtakes her.

I felt cheated that she has monopolized the conversation. I thought we would share a quiet bond, but I had no commonality with her story of blame. I am not out to prove anything or to get anything back. As she talks, I begin to feel light leeching away from my glass.

I try to keep my expression neutral, but it's difficult because my feelings differ so sharply from hers. It seems she is trying to outsource her share of the pain, conveniently overlooking or dismissing the fact that I have sorrows and difficulties of my own. She seems bound to the past, trapped in some kind of entitled role of victim. Others owe her for her loss. She continues on for twenty or so minutes. I feel sorry for her—for her loss but more so for her reaction to it. Boiling water doesn't allow reflections. She does not realize the insights and divine connections she is forfeiting.

As I drive home, I think about why dying has such different effects on people. Dying is more than the simple act of leaving this earth and exiting the body. Death has a message attached to it. It is a final moment that seems capable of binding others to us and setting them free at the same time. A good death does this. Sometimes there is the knowledge that an earthly exit is imminent. This can provide an opportunity to generously leave loved ones with good memories and hopes.

This is why suicide has thorns. This type of death can carry a message of anger or shame—a feeling of deceitful departure accompanied by lifelong doubts. The manner of death really does influence the heart of those left behind. It is the final, summing-up scene of life. If the manner of death is consistent in character, beliefs, and purpose, then those left behind feel unity and peace. But if the means of death diverges from long-held beliefs and character, those left behind struggle to complete the story of who this person really was.

I see this mother struggling to complete her son's story, pulling in audience members to play roles they never really had.

I arrive home off-kilter, not sure what to do with the feelings that are jangling around inside of me and emotionally thrown by the lack of expected empathy. I lie down on my bed and open up my computer. I start scanning down through some notes I have made and come across a way to recycle this debris. It's from a blog I read many years ago.

The writer, a mother, is listening to her daughter tell about an emotionally damaging interaction with another child at school that day. The mother explains to her daughter that every person in our lives serves a purpose. They teach us either what *to* do or what *not* to do. She tells her daughter to consider the encounters we have with others. When someone hurts our feelings, we should lean into those feelings and ask ourselves what they did that made us feel that way. Was it the words they chose? Their tone? Whatever they did gives us an opportunity to make ourselves better with a pledge. This is how we learn from others' mistakes.

She reminds her daughter that no one can meet all our needs, but everyone has something to offer. Look at every person as someone here to teach something. After she asks her daughter what she learned from the painful experience, the following exchange takes place:

> My daughter thought for a moment. Then she said, "To be happy for other people's good news and not be jealous. To say something comforting when people tell me they are scared or when they share bad news."
>
> "Yes, exactly!" I said. "I'm very sorry you had that experience today. It doesn't sound like that friend is going to change anytime soon, but all hope it not lost — you can be the change!" . . .
>
> I told her it might be a good idea to make a pledge of what she's going to do. . . .
>
> We came home and made a pledge notebook. We both agreed to use it whenever an unlikely "teacher" taught us something through a hurtful experience.[31]

As I read over these notes, I feel my glass turn solar, drawing all kinds of sunlight in and transforming and storing it for future uses. This is definitely the message I needed to hear—not only today but for all the times that insensitive or inappropriate things are said to me, which is beginning to happen more often now. I understand why grievers pull away from society. Too many people ask tactless questions and give wounding advice.

In the past, my heart could only discern a small bandwidth of light. But now, because of my glass, my heart seems to operate on the entire spectrum from infrared to ultraviolet, offering me an abundant range of responses—most not customary to this world.

I pull out my journal and write the following:

- I pledge to never blame anyone for Brieson's death.
- I pledge to share my experiences, not off-load them.

---

31. Rachel Macy Stafford, "An Empowering Way to Respond to Hurtful People," Medium, Apr. 27, 2017, https://medium.com/thrive-global/an-empowering-way-to-respond-to-hurtful-people-fb83583d9d19.

- I pledge to keep my heart open and aware of those who suffer and not become so submerged in my own grief that I cannot feel the vibrations of another's pain.
- I pledge to never be angry about what has happened.
- I pledge to be compassionate before curious.
- I pledge to never force a confidence.
- I pledge to care more for others than whether others care for me.

It's not a profound list, and it says less than I have learned. But in this moment, it comes to me that carrying grief might involve some actual skills and not simply religious beliefs.[32] I recognize that many people have helped me along this path with their spiritual gifts. I wonder if it's possible to share these ideas with others. A grief seminar perhaps? Just as quickly, I dismiss it. Who would attend? People have a natural aversion to darkness and loss.

It does seem that darkness tempts us to focus on the wrong things though. If we don't have light within us, then when these challenging and heavy emotions come, we try to create some kind of artificial light to keep them at bay—things like binge watching, compulsive scrolling, drugs, alcohol, meaningless sex, manic busyness, and so on. Even emotions as simple as jealousy can be pushed aside or buried using these distractions.

I have found that these dark and complex emotions I have been experiencing actually reveal something about myself that I needed to know. When properly met, they have awakened my heart, opened my mind, and changed my inner essence. They carry more muscle than any carefree encounter ever has. Mourning is a purposeful mechanism for self-discovery.

---

32. As journalist Germany Kent put it, "The world is not interested in the people who've done you wrong or your struggles, but rather how you have reacted and dealt with the wrongs that have been done to you" (Goodreads, accessed Aug. 21, 2023, https://www.goodreads.com/quotes/10086131-the-world-is-not-interested-in-the-people-who-ve-done).

Day 305: The Gift of Majestic Perspective

THINGS ARE NO SOONER PLEDGED THAN THEY ARE TESTED. ONE OF my friends tells someone, "Shelly is over it already. It must not have been too surprising for her."

Apparently, she believes that what she personally witnesses is all there is to my grief. I am reminded of a scene from *Sense and Sensibility*, a story that Jane Austen wrote dealing with this very subject: public and private grief. This story is about two sisters, Marianne and Elinor. Each sister suffers a disillusioning heartbreak.

Marianne, the younger sister, believes she has experienced the ultimate grief. She thrashes, she cries, she mopes, and she causes as much trouble as she can. She receives sympathy and solicitations. Everyone handles her with kid gloves. Instead of this sympathy alleviating her, it seems to increase Marianne's throes of sorrow until she actually makes herself sick with this grief, nearly dying in the process.

Meanwhile, Elinor, her sister, also carries heavy disappointments, difficult situations, and heartbreak. She feels them just as much as Marianne, but she keeps those emotions private in an effort to spare those around her. She struggles against the pain and accepts and submits. She appears cheerful and helpful, always doing her part.

When Marianne discovers that Elinor has been carrying these disappointments without any public displays, she can't understand how someone can be grieving and not emoting. "Elinor, where is your heart?" she demands.

In reply, Elinor's astonishment is evident as she grapples with how to explain her feelings to Marianne: "What do you know of my heart? . . . For weeks . . . I have had this pressing on me without being at liberty to speak of it to a single creature. . . . Believe me, Marianne, had I not been bound to silence I could have produced proof enough of a broken heart even for you."[33]

Later Marianne recognizes the generosity of Elinor's response. She has come to realize that curling in upon oneself stops the conduit for receiving. Then, despite how others may try, they cannot reach our void, and any trickle that does get through has a tenuous hold—it doesn't last long.

I have found that if I turn first to God and remain accessible to Him, I feel anchored on something real and solid, and others' gestures of compassion land on fertile soil. The ground even becomes holy. But if I try to let others pave my path for me, I find the way overgrown with weeds and the moments of compassion choked before they can sprout.

I have to do much clearing of undergrowth as I go along. There are many things inside of me that need dug up or plowed under. But as I traverse this barely distinguishable path, it has begun to feel oddly familiar, as if I once walked here every day as a carefree child.

The path is not an easy stroll—it has a steep incline. But I know I do not need to conquer the entire mountain of grief right now. I don't have to have everything figured out today in order to take a step forward. I don't consider the elevation or the gradient; I just remind myself that every mountain gets climbed one step at a time. I take frequent breaks, look back where I've been, and try to value this new viewpoint. I know the rest will come in time. For now, it's just about taking that next step. I have faith that someday this mountain before me will be a peak beneath me.

Day 309: The Gift of Favor

I DECIDE TO START READING THE BOOK OF MORMON WHILE MARK-ing and studying all the passages that speak of grief or mourning.

---

33. *Sense and Sensibility*, directed by Ang Lee (Colombia Pictures, 1995). Screenplay script found at https://imsdb.com/scripts/Sense-and-Sensibility. html.

I am only one verse in when I encounter this: "Having seen many afflictions in the course of my days, nevertheless, having been highly favored of the Lord in all my days" (1 Nephi 1:1).

In all my days? Even when Nephi has to leave behind all his wealth and inheritance to travel for years through the wilderness? Even when he is beaten by his brothers? Even when he is bound by heavy cords? Even when everyone is angry that he broke his bow? Even when his father dies? Even when he has to separate himself from his brothers?

In fact, now that I'm thinking about it . . . when *was* the good part? It seems Nephi spent most of his life in afflictions of one kind or another. How does he say he is highly favored of the Lord?

Peter tells us that the Lord does not play favorites: "Of a truth I perceive that God is no respecter of persons: but in every nation he that feareth him, and worketh righteousness, is accepted of him" (Acts 10:35).

After the most cursory study, I realize I am seeing it wrong.

Favoritism is the practice of giving unfair preferential treatment to one person or group at the expense of another. God certainly does not do this. He is just. Unfair preferential treatment is not in His nature. However, God does favor people. And *favored* means endowed with special gifts or talents.

These gifts come with assignments or responsibilities—situations God offers us and we choose to pick up. I can reject these situations— push them aside like Laman and Lemuel—or I can choose to shoulder them as Nephi did. In so doing, God endows us with special gifts. I know this is true. I have experienced it daily—truly daily.

I have been given strength, qualities, understanding, and support to face the tasks I have been given or that have fallen to my lot. Or perhaps I have just been provided with the greatest gift—the constant companionship of the Holy Ghost—and this brings a multiplicity of benefits.

As an understanding of what Nephi has written settles over me, I experience what I often feel when studying God's word: a reset button has been quietly pushed, a misconception has been cleared, my belief system has been rebooted. I now have a stronger connection than before.

Day 327: The Gift of Restoring

JOEY AND I PICK UP KELLEE FROM THE AIRPORT. WE LAUGH AS SHE walks within two feet of us, texting us but never seeing us. We shout and wave, but she walks right by. It's the perfect start to a hilarious day—my favorite kind of day. We are headed to goat yoga.

If I could choose any two people in the entire world to try this activity with, it would be Kellee and Joey. They are both acrobatic and outrageous—the two requirements for this sport. We take loads of pictures and have more funny moments than you would think is possible with just a goat and some food pellets. I don't think the yoga instructors are especially thrilled with us. They seem to skirt around us as often as possible. We laugh and laugh as the antics escalate.

This is a unique gift. Although everyone will give me sympathy—even complete strangers will offer it to me—I have few people who will laugh with me during grief. Kellee and Joey have just my kind of humor and know just how to administer the dosage in precise increments for maximum effect.

Being in their presence helps me forget the burden altogether. The pain seems strangely distant and easily manageable. I am encouraged—given courage—as they instill energy that was beginning to flag. Being with them does not change the burden; it changes *me*. Few people do I trust well enough to allow that.

They treat me as if I am still me, even when I have not been me for a long time—so long that I even forget who I was. But because they have been the witnesses of my life, even the writers of it sometimes, they know the character I portray and can keep the plot going even when I have lost the script. I have missed my friends, missed these moments, missed myself.

Through the laughter and through the antics, little pieces of who I am fall back into place.

Day 331: Pennies

My youngest daughter, Siearra, has her twentieth birthday today. I call her at college to wish her a happy birthday and to make sure she got my package. During the course of the conversation, she says, "Mom, I've been finding pennies all week."

"Really?" I inquire, unsure what she's saying.

"Yes, seven days ago, while getting out of my car, I looked down and saw a bejeweled *B* lying on the ground. I picked it up thinking, 'Oh, a *B* for Brieson.' I put it in my jacket. Then every day since then, I have found a penny on the ground. Every single day. Mom, I know they were reminders from Brieson because my birthday was coming up."

Brieson was a conscientious gift giver, spending great amounts of time and effort to pick something he felt the receiver would both need and enjoy—usually something unexpected and unique. Even the wrapping had to be perfectly chosen.

Not sure what to say, I simply agree with Siearra that finding pennies on the ground in a snowy environment would be unusual, especially to find seven in seven consecutive days. I ask her what she thinks it means.

She replies, "I'm not sure—just that Brieson is watching out for me I guess."

Christine has had similar experiences with pennies. She says that all the pennies she finds are old and beat-up and only appear when she is doing something that she knows Brieson would like to be involved in or when she has been especially upset by something. She says they seem to appear out of thin air sometimes. Christine believes Brieson leaves the pennies to let her know he is still part of her life—still around and aware of her.

I have never found a penny, but I feel a confirming relief: I am not the only one receiving messages. Others are sensing his communications as well. A sense of holiness wells up inside of me, but I also can't help wondering why I have never received a penny.

Day 334: My Penny

GRIEF SOMETIMES FEELS LIKE A KNIFE THAT HAS BEEN CAREFULLY slid between my ribs. Most of the time the jagged edges don't hurt because it is lodged so tightly that it has almost become a part of me. But every once in a while, someone will accidentally jar the handle, and then the pain is quite breathtaking.

After our team lesson this morning, a few of us stay to play an additional set before we meet up again for lunch. We remain on the same court that we have been using for the last hour. We finish our set and still have some time before we need to leave, so we sit on the bench and just chat.

At one point, the conversation turns to Elvis. One of the ladies said, "Well, then he had to go and kill himself!" There is a moment of stunned silence as both she and everyone else realize what she has said—and in whose presence. Rona meets my eyes across the words.

I am disconcerted and a little shaken, as one always is with sudden pain. I twist on the bench and finger my ribs, stilling the shuddering handle. I try to keep my face neutral, but I must have betrayed my hurt. There is a deep, awkward pause for just a few beats, then Rona picks up the conversation and turns it away. I say nothing at all. This woman has always been very kind to me. I know she didn't mean to say what she did, but still, my heart is hanging by gristle.

A few moments later, we gather our equipment and prepare to leave for lunch. I walk around the bench and my eyes fall on a scuffed-up penny lying just in front of the bench. I have walked back and forth across this very area at least twelve or more times today, but only now do I see this penny sitting in full view on the court.

The others have walked on ahead of me toward the clubhouse. I bend down and pick the penny up, turning it over. Everyone is talking and laughing as I trail a few feet behind, swallowing down a little gulp of sadness. The penny fits easily into my palm—as if it is something to wield—and a strange sense of empowerment is pushed straight into my bloodstream. My ribs seem to adjust, soften, and flex around my jagged glass. I take a deep breathe. Everything is fine.

God has His own timing. If I'm honest with myself, in the past I have always felt that God was mostly dragging His feet about answering me. But I can see now that God was often early in responding to my needs—I just didn't give Him the credit. Instead, I chalked it up to a fortuitous happenstance or a lucky break. Only when God has made me wait—made me work—have I acknowledged His hand in the solution. God being early is taken for granted, and I can see why He is careful to give me experiences that don't allow me to forget Him. That's why my penny miracle had to come *after* I wanted it.

I feel as if God will answer any strange request I throw out. People often answer my requests too. I worry I might get selfish. I might try to take advantage of this freely given compassion to my own detriment. It seems gifts come so easily and so willingly, with hardly any effort at all from me.

Day 364: The Gift of Group Commemoration

TOMORROW IS THE ONE-YEAR MARK. I CAN'T HELP BUT THINK BACK to one year ago today: Brieson's last day as a person on this earth and my last day as the person I once was. That day I was also on my way to tennis, just like I am today. Looking back, it seems I was standing on top of the world, looking out on a thriving forest. Today that same view seems scorched and gray.

One entire year later and here I am, headed to the same facility, to do the same activity, in the same weather. My exterior activities are practically identical to what they were a year ago, but my interior motions have become radically transformed. All the things I do now are the exact same things I have always done but dustier—smoke-damaged perhaps.

Julie has invited some team members to play today. Knowing Julie, I should have suspected something, but I don't. I have no expectations that anyone will remember. Why would they? I have said nothing about the one-year anniversary, and no one has mentioned it.

After we play for a few hours, we are talking by the side of the courts. I am sitting next to Karen. Julie stands up and says, "We want to present something to you." She looks in my direction.

Since Karen is new to the team and has been such a valuable addition, I assume it's about her. I look to my right to see Karen's reaction. But Karen is looking right back at me, and I startle to realize that this is about me!

I turn back to Julie as she continues: "We know it's been one year since your son died, and we want you to know we are with you in all of this and love you." She hands me a poster. I unroll it to find a collage of memorable and funny images. I laugh at each one. This team really does get me.

In that moment I feel as if I have turned a corner and am no longer headed toward that scorched and smoky landscape. Instead, I am leaving that behind, and a fresh breeze is whipping up the ashes and blowing them away.

The team has also compiled short messages from each person. Joey quotes C. S. Lewis in her note: "Friendship is unnecessary, like philosophy, like art. . . . It has no survival value; rather it is one of those things that give value to survival."[34] I couldn't agree more.

Day 365a: The Gift of Divine Messages

I HAVE BEEN PREPARING FOR THIS DAY. I FEEL CERTAIN IT WILL BE heavy with sorrowful memories and lost future expectations. My husband has taken the day off work, or maybe he already had the day off since it was a Friday. Either way, we plan to spend the morning at an Arizona Phoenix Mission zone conference.

I am still a little confused as to why we are invited to this. After all, I only do the mission newsletter, a peripheral job at best. I am not really involved in the missionary work or anything related to the

---

34. Ariadne Lewis and Annie Dawson, "What Is Friendship?," Geneva College, accessed Aug. 21, 2023, https://www.geneva.edu/academics/crossroads/geneva-question/what-is-friendship.

mission directly. There is no reason at all for my husband to attend, but he does. We drive to Camelback Road where the conference will be held.

Upon arriving at the church building, we are greeted by Scott and Gayla, and when we look around, we realize they are the only people we know here. We choose a seat on the third row and sit down. After a few minutes, Elder Mark Frost, an Area Seventy, enters the room. We have not seen or talked to him since the day he gave us a priesthood blessing almost ten months ago. He talks to a few people at the back, and I expect him to wave to us as he continues up to the stand. He has his special needs son with him and has many people vying for his attention.

He shakes a few hands on his way to the front, but instead of just waving at us, he walks all the way down our row to personally greet us. He says, "I was hoping you would come today. I've been thinking about you."

I'm surprised by this since there really isn't a reason for us to be here today. I feel my glass blink on and stay red. As I consider this further, I decide he is just expressing a social kindness that he's probably said to many. I am reading too much into it. During most of the meeting, my mind keeps circling back to Brieson.

The meeting begins with the stake president telling about how the inner-city mission began and about its purpose. Several others speak, but I don't remember who they are or what they say. Then Elder Frost gets up. He begins with a common introduction of expressing appreciation for all the people attending and sharing his hope that he would say something of worth. Then he pauses. For just a fraction of a second, he looks up, right at me, and says, "I have been praying that you would be here today." I felt that piercing sensation when you know that something said generally was meant with specificity, and the arrow hits its mark.

His talk is about being numbered unto the Lord—the value of knowing and numbering those we serve. Of course, any message about numbers is fascinating to me, especially if it has religious connotations. I listen intently and take careful notes. I remember something that Elder Frost said to me once, several years ago, in a private meeting: "Shelly, although the Church has millions of members, the Lord knows the one." At the time it brought immediate tears to my eyes, and this message adds layers to that moment.

After the closing prayer, there's a dinner. Since we have few acquaintances in the group, and the three we do know are in high demand, we go directly to the cultural hall and start down the food line. We choose a table near the back and sit down. As we eat, dozens of other missionaries load up their plates and sit at other tables. The tables are filling up, but our table remains mostly empty. Finally, as almost the very last person, Elder Frost enters the room. He and his son get their food. Many people have finished their meals by this time and have left. There are many empty seats around the room now—many places he could sit—but he comes straight over and sits down next to us.

After settling his son and talking with a few people who have followed him to our table, he asks, "How are you doing? I have been thinking about calling you, but I keep forgetting until it's too late to call."

We respond with set phrases: "We're doing good. Thank you."

He is interrupted by a steady stream of people coming up to shake his hand or ask him a question or just remind him of a common acquaintance. We get dessert and talk with the others now sitting at our table.

After about ten minutes, Elder Frost is able to begin eating. We all eat in silence for about a minute, and then he leans forward and asks, "How *are* you doing?" He then pauses and seems to consider something. Then, looking up directly at me, he says, "Today is the anniversary of his death."

I am sure my jaw dropped. "Yes, it is," I reply, "I can't believe you know that!" I am wide with astonishment. How did he know this? I feel the presence of God descend on me—not just His presence but His full, single-minded attention.

Although I had asked Elder Frost to come and give my husband and me a blessing, this happened several weeks after Brieson's death and funeral. I am certain we never told him the date of his death. I am completely astounded—speechless. How did he know? How did he remember something he was never told?

Elder Frost doesn't respond. He just gently looks at me with a steady gaze. I take a big deep breath as this feeling of being watched over—carefully tended to—engulfs me.

If I have ever had doubts about whether God is sending messengers, this moment incinerated those doubts to ashes. Clearly heaven has not forgotten the anniversary of this difficult day. And to preclude any chance I have of missing the message that heaven is aware of me, God sent a special servant to deliver it straight to me. There can be no mistaking the matter. It is irrefutable proof.

Day 374: The Gift of Prophecy

SOMETIMES I CAN SEE A BAD DAY COMING AT ME LIKE A DUST STORM. Far off on the horizon, I feel its gritty approach. This morning, I wake with a feeling 180 degrees from that—an impression of coming clarity. Far off on the horizon, something is coming. Part of this is because it's general conference weekend. I always look forward to this; it always brings some new insights.

Yesterday was a significant session. We sustained a new First Presidency and two new members of the Quorum of the Twelve Apostles. The priesthood quorums were combined into one elders quorum. If that wasn't enough, President Nelson also announced that ministering would replace home and visiting teaching. Usually change happens quite slowly, but President Nelson is certainly taking to heart the phrase "hasten the work."

The morning and afternoon sessions are filled with more things to consider and more adjustments to make. This is, without question, the most surprising and newsworthy conference I have ever heard. I am still trying to take in all the restructuring and changes that are happening when President Nelson stands up to make concluding remarks, so I almost miss his crowning encore. He says, "Our message to the world is simple and sincere: We invite all of God's children on both sides of the veil to come unto their Savior, receive the blessings of the holy temple, have enduring joy, and qualify for eternal life."[35]

Electricity shoots through me: "Invite *all* of God's *children* on *both* sides of the veil to come unto their Savior, receive the blessings of the holy temple, have enduring *joy* and *qualify* for eternal life."

It's a little moment of transfiguration. These are all the things I wish for Brieson. It's as if President Nelson, hearing the faint whisperings of my heart, could not let conference end without sending me assurances that those who are gone from this life are not forgotten. He gently gathered up my smudged and blotchy yearnings, wiped off the doubt, and handed them back to me shiny new.

I felt as if something that had been slowly gaining on me all day had finally caught up to me. For a few steps, it matched me stride for stride and then shot off into the distance ahead.

Day 384: The Gift of Opportunities to Serve

AFTER MUCH CONSIDERATION, WE DECIDE TO VOLUNTEER TO BE leadership support missionaries in the Arizona Phoenix Stake. We have been looking for some way to contribute—some way to feel productive. Although this opportunity has been presented a few times to us, I have been reluctant to do it. It doesn't seem like anything I would have experience or gifts to do.

But then one afternoon, while Stacey is on a business trip to China, I call up Scott, a member of the mission presidency, and ask for some details. Everything immediately falls into place within days—hours almost. We meet with the stake president, and he assigns us to the Rose Lane Ward.

The Tuckers are leaving within the week, and they quickly update and train us. They take us around the ward each night explaining who they are working with, and we watch them teach several investigators.

---

35. Russell M. Nelson, "Let Us All Press On," *Ensign* or *Liahona*, May 2018, 118–19.

We have the missionaries with us as well: Elder Richardson and Elder Eilers. I feel a little out of my element since I never went on a mission and don't even know the order of the lessons.

I watch as the Tuckers teach Johnny Gutierrez's grandchildren. It's chaos. They're running in and out, jumping on the couches, fighting with each other. It's a wonder they hear anything. Then Sister Tucker asks a question about the plan of salvation. Alexis, age 13, calm as can be, starts to explain the main points to her. Her words carry more than just memorized phrases—she is really thinking about what she's saying, trying to articulate what she believes. I have an overwhelming urge to stop the lesson, and I do. I ask Alexis how she knows this. Alexis just shrugs, unsure how to articulate her knowledge.

I feel a big lift after we leave—excitement that there is so much opportunity. I feel an immediate connection to this family, as if we have been sent for this express purpose—to meet them. This opportunity is life-changing, life-saving, life-enhancing. I love every minute of the time I will spend with the members of this ward. I glean much more than I give.

It's funny how I think I'm an expert of my own happiness—that I know exactly what I need to be perfectly, blissfully happy. Then when I get it, I spike and plummet right back to discontent. Or sometimes, like today, I get something I have never considered as an avenue for happiness, but it brings a molecular bliss.

Day 412: The Gift of Keys

I READ THIS FAMILIAR STORY AGAIN TODAY, BUT AS OFTEN HAPPENS now, the script becomes bolded and luminous.

> [Jesus] saith unto them, But whom say ye that I am?
>
> And Simon Peter answered and said, Thou art the Christ, the Son of the living God.
>
> And Jesus answered and said unto him, Blessed art thou, Simon Bar-jona: for flesh and blood hath not revealed it unto thee, but my Father which is in heaven.

And I say also unto thee, That thou art Peter, and upon this rock I will build my church; and the gates of hell shall not prevail against it.

And I will give unto thee the keys of the kingdom of heaven: and whatsoever thou shalt bind on earth shall be bound in heaven: and whatsoever thou shalt loose on earth shall be loosed in heaven. (Matthew 16:15–19)

I search further and find this: "And again I say unto you, ye must repent, and be baptized in my name, and become as a little child, or ye can in nowise inherit the kingdom of God. Verily, verily, I say unto you, that this is my doctrine, and whoso buildeth upon this buildeth upon my rock, and the gates of hell shall not prevail against them" (3 Nephi 11:38–39).

I have always assumed this meant that the gates of hell won't be able to keep someone in hell—that hell can't have power greater than your power. But today I wondered if it might work the other way as well. If one has kept the commandments and followed Christ, then surely the gates of hell are not more powerful than your force—you can enter hell and walk right back out again. Those gates have no control over your entrance or departure. You may come and go as you please.

I think about that second day when our doorknob broke (see "Day 2b"). Doors or gates in the Bible are places of sacrifice and judgment—places that require keys, special permission, or authority to enter.[36]

Wouldn't someone unlocking and walking through those gates, intent on sharing all the wonders outside those gates, be irresistible to

---

36. There are numerous keys mentioned in scripture, and maybe they all unlock the gates of hell: the key of death and hell (see Revelation 1:18); the key of knowledge (see Luke 11:52); the key to the bottomless pit (see Revelations 9:1); and keys listed throughout Doctrine and Covenants 107.

those within the gates? Especially if it were someone they loved and trusted?[37]

Day 449: Bulletproof Glass

I'M AT TENNIS PLAYING A FRIENDLY GAME WITH SOME LADIES. WE stop between sets to take a break. One of the ladies says, "Have you heard about Kate Spade?"

Strangely enough, I haven't heard. I barely recognize the name. My mind is spinning, trying to remember why it sounds familiar. I'm sitting across the table from her, and I look right at her and innocently ask, "No, what about her?"

In that moment her face blanches, and instinctively I know it's about suicide. She looks down. But another lady, standing behind me, doesn't see her reaction. So she answers me: "She committed suicide!"

She continues, her voice rising. "My daughter wanted to go out and buy a Kate Spade purse as a kind of memorial to her. I told her, 'Oh no! We don't want to associate ourselves with that.'"

I meet eyes with my friend across the wrought iron table, which seems to be gradually widening between us. I feel like the first time I was thrown from a horse: flailing and grappling and then the ground rushing up to meet me. Then, as now, I could do nothing to prevent the shock that was coming.

Now I'm blushing—embarrassed for myself, for the others, for the awkwardness of the situation, and for the moment of revelation that must certainly follow this conversation.

---

37. Fyodor Dostoevsky wrote: "What is hell? I think it is the suffering of one who can no longer love" (*Brothers Karamazov* [New York: Random House Publishing, 2003], 431). Also, years later, in October 2020, President Nelson gave a talk titled "Let God Prevail." In that talk, he cautions us about being "myopic" and instead letting God prevail. When I look up the definition of *myopic*, I realize I have been "lacking in imagination, foresight, or intellectual insight" about so many things, especially in regard to eternal progression.

Then just as suddenly, my glass, which I am expecting to be pulsing with pain, instead turns bulletproof. The ladies continue talking, even jumping in over the top of each other, but I can't hear what they say because the world around me has muted and a kind of wordless conversation seems to take place within me. The scene around me goes into slow motion as my glass absorbs the negative energy.

First, there's a chloroforming of the shame, and then a spiritual anesthesia fills me with a heart-swelling elation and pure happiness. Right there, in the midst of a condemning conversation, I feel God's buffering presence so strongly that I am fully distanced from what is being said. I never hear their opinions or their conclusions. I go from feeling like a suspicious character who should be placed under surveillance to being given gold-card status, waved through a gate, and invited into the elite lounge.

It was a hard moment, but I have learned that all stepping stones come mixed with hard elements; it is what gives the step stability. No one wants to step up onto a shaky surface. The concrete—the hard moment that takes some time to settle—allows me to step up to a wider perspective. To this day, I don't know anything else about that conversation. I literally did not hear a single word of it.[38]

As I stand up to go back onto the court, I feel so light that my feet nearly leave the ground. I know that no matter how often suicide is talked about in my presence, I have the foundation to hear it.

---

38. Later I read this quote by Craig D. Lounsbrough on an Instagram post: "I am wholly deserving of all the consequences that I will in fact never receive simply because God unashamedly stepped in front of me on the cross, unflinchingly spread His arms so as to completely shield me from the retribution that was mine to bear, and repeatedly took the blows. And I stand entirely unwounded, utterly lost in the fact that the while His body was pummeled and bloodied to death by that which was meant for me and me alone, I have not a scratch" (Goodreads, accessed Aug. 21, 2023, https://www.goodreads.com/quotes/6799530-i-am-wholly-deserving-of-all-the-consequences-that-i).

Day 484: The Gift of Unknown Stories

BRIESON HAD SEVERAL COLLEGE FRIENDS, SOME OF WHOM I HEARD about and met. But I never visited Brieson at college. That world was completely separate from his world here.

Several of his friends from college decide to write down memories of Brieson. The Bowns sisters find photos and compile all of them into a book. Today I receive this gift in the mail.

The book is filled with Brieson—stories I have never heard, pictures I have never seen, of a place and a time of which I had no part. As I read through the stories, my tears well up, and through blurry eyes, who he is comes into sharper focus.

I didn't realize how starved for details I am. There are parts of his life that I have only the barest inkling of regarding what he did, who he was with, and how he acted. This new information gives me something from which to draw strength. He affected others' lives for good, and they have not forgotten. These details add fodder to my hope. After all, even faith as strong as Nephi's needed some tender mercies from time to time.

One of the problems with suicide is that people can reduce his whole life to this one incident. It tends to overshadow every other event of his life. For some, this will always be the window through which they will view Brieson—it's easy to do. And that is why this is such a stunning gift. Those friends understand this principle: that "when someone takes their own life, only God is able to judge their thoughts, their actions, and their level of accountability. Suicide need not be the defining characteristic of an individual's eternal life."[39]

Innately, these friends understand the importance of remembering him as the fuller person. They want me to know they remember *all* of Brieson—the complete Brieson. He isn't just a life that ended. He is a life that continues to affect them. This quiets my niggling fear

---

39. "Suicide: Doctrines and Principles," The Church of Jesus Christ of Latter-day Saints, accessed Aug. 21, 2023, https://www.churchofjesuschrist.org/study/manual/suicide-doctrine-and-principles/doctrine-and-principles?lang=eng.

that one day I will wake up and my son will be a stranger, even to me. These details and pictures make him more vivid than ever.

This small photo album provides me with fresh insight. One of the strangest aspects of loss is that I have learned more things about Brieson after his death than I knew when he was alive. I see him from angles that were never shared with me previously. His life had narrowed so much in that last year. He rarely went anywhere or did anything except with a small selection of people. Now here I am, being given a gift of comprehension into who he was at his happiest time.

A soft understanding settles over me that something new is being created with his life. Although things seem to have unraveled, there is still enough good experiences to allow a restoration. It's a sort of reknitting or weaving, creating a seamless bridge across gaps of time and knowledge—so strong that it can uphold his life's weight.

Day 508: The Gift of Bringing Along

I WAKE UP NOT KNOWING WHAT I WILL DO OR WHERE I WILL GO. I'M not exactly down, but that doesn't mean I'm up. "Not down" doesn't equate to "up." Sometimes it just means a kind of holding pattern: coping, I guess. But coping is not enjoying.

Bing. A text from Angleina: "I know this is last minute, but I was wondering if you would like to come with me this morning (at 9:30) to the scripture study class at the stake center . . ."

I reply, "It's a possibility."

I try to decide if I'm up for this. Do I want to go? It's so much easier to lie here and just wrap myself in this bed. There's really no reason to go. She won't care if I make an excuse and tell her I have something else planned. It's partly true: I plan to stay blighted all day.

The jagged glass spurs me: *Get up.*

I roll out of bed and text Angleina back: "Ok. I'm available to go. Sounds fun." She offers to pick me up—a second level of invite. Otherwise, I might have wavered and decided not to go. Accepting the ride means I'm committed.

As the teacher, Charlotte, begins the class, it seems as if I'm watching everything from below a soggy surface. There's a kind of natural barrier between me and this world. I'm far underwater, and things are different down here—quite different. I clearly remember the sunshine overhead; I can even see it glancing off the shallows above me. I can sense everyone around me still lightheartedly splashing in the waves while undercurrents are pulling at me.

Yet I have to acknowledge that even with the apparent lack of oxygen, I am floating peacefully in this subterranean realm. As long as I don't resist, I'm carried along. It's events like this that add inner buoyancy to me. As this realization comes to me, I seem to float smoothly from coping to savoring. I don't want this class to ever end.

But it does end, and Pam comes up to talk to me. I recall a verse that I wanted to share with her. I hunt through my scriptures until I find it: "For behold, the promises which we have obtained are promises unto us according to the flesh; wherefore, as it has been shown unto me that many of our children shall perish in the flesh because of unbelief, nevertheless, God will be merciful unto many; and our children shall be restored, that they may come to that which will give them the true knowledge of their Redeemer" (2 Nephi 10:2).

Pam says, "I want that scripture. Will you send it to me?" I realize that everyone, no matter how long ago their loss, still looks for those messages, the reassurances, the little understandings.

As we drive back home, I thank Angleina for thinking of me. She confesses that she was hesitant to invite me on such short notice, but she's glad she did.

I smile to myself. *Here is Angleina thinking she's bothering me when actually she's rescuing me. Today feels as if she has offered me the last seat in a life raft on the Titanic. Sometimes the difference is hard to discern: annoying or saving?* In reality, it can be both. Like I said, miracles can bother people.[40]

---

40. See "Looking Back: Miracles" on page 3 of this book.

Day 641: The Gift of Christmas Wishes

LAST CHRISTMAS ALL OF OUR CHILDREN CAME; THIS YEAR THEY didn't. It's the first Christmas with only Siearra, and it feels very lonely and blank. I can't remember Christmas Eve in decades without any little kids around. We have no family parties or events this year. The whole season has gone by without any real celebration. I'm just waiting for tomorrow to be over so I can pack up the tree.

Last night Stacey and I watched *It's a Wonderful Life.* I had forgotten that George Bailey wanted to commit suicide by jumping off a bridge. If you remember the story, Clarence, an angel, is assigned to show George what the world would be like if he had never been born. George struggles to believe that Clarence is who he says he is. At one point, Clarence pointedly asks George, "Don't you believe in angels?"

George retorts, "Well, sure I do."

Clarence replies in the most matter-of-fact tone imaginable: "If you believe in angels, then why are you so surprised when you see one?"

Tonight, we are watching *Daddy's Home 2.* It's a comedy and one of my all-time favorites. I am fully involved in it when suddenly I feel a creeping melancholy begin to eat away at the edges of my enjoyment and my mind is pulled back to George Bailey.

I lay down on the couch and stop attending to the movie at all. I am thinking about what Judgment Day will be like. *Do we get to see what impact we had on others? Do we see exactly how our lives mattered? Did it have an effect? Was it important?*

I am getting more emotional and don't want Christmas Eve to be ruined by my upheaval, and so to distract myself, I pick up my phone. There are no text messages, but I have one email. I click on it. It's a text, sent over email from Cami:

"Just want you to know that we are thinking about your sweet Brieson tonight. The song 'All I Want for Christmas Is You' just came on the radio, and Ali said this song will always remind her of Brieson. They used to sing it all the time. Love that boy of yours who will always be thought of by the Blair Family. Merry Christmas."

When I read the words "All I Want for Christmas Is You," my heart becomes wildly erratic, first jumping into my throat and then plunging toward my stomach.

It's uncanny how often this happens. It's been almost two years, and these things still happen with such reliable regularity that it just *has* to be Spirit-driven. No one can be this attentive, can they?

Cami sends this message as if it's the most common thing imaginable to text someone on Christmas Eve telling them she is thinking about their twenty-five-year-old son. The timing and message are piercing.

I guess I identify with George Bailey more than I realized. I am still reluctant to believe that my ordinary life is worthy of angelic intervention.

Day 667: The Gift of Paying It Forward

WHILE RANDOMLY SCROLLING THROUGH THE INTERNET A FEW DAYS ago, I noticed that January 18th is National Winnie the Pooh Day. My glass presses into me—a sharp little punch.

Elizabeth Poots, a young woman in Rose Lane Ward who died of cancer about a month ago, was a lover of all things Winnie the Pooh. I gave her an Eeyore onesie and a Winnie the Pooh watch for her birthday.

In November, just a few days after her birthday, she checked into the hospital. On our way home from a baptism, my husband and I stopped in to see her. There was no one in her room—just a sign saying she had gone for some testing. We left a note and a small toy. The next day she passed away.

I continue scrolling, but my glass won't let up. It prods at me: *Do something!* I look at my watch. The holiday is three days away. What could I possibly do on such short notice? I know that her mother, Katherine, is suffering. It's only been weeks since her funeral.

I stop scrolling, open up a new document, and start designing an invitation with no real idea in mind. I'm just looking for Winnie the

Pooh quotes. The first one to pop up says, "Nobody can be uncheered with a balloon." Inspiration strikes and sticks. I know what to do.

I invite all the women in the ward to a commemorative balloon launch in honor of Elizabeth on National Winnie the Pooh Day.

The day arrives rather quickly. First, I pick up Kellee from the airport, then we buy thirty balloons. I also have tags and pens to attach messages to the balloons. I have a few doubts about the attendance and wonder if it will just be Kellee, the full-time elders, the Relief Society president, and me.

Upon arrival I'm heartened and relieved to see a battalion of over fifteen people waiting by the picnic tables. Katherine was not among them, but I knew from Lynette's example (see "Day 7b") that she didn't need to be physically there to benefit from this show of support. We quickly gather. I read a few quotes from Winnie the Pooh that seem especially made for this day:

- "Love is taking a few steps backward, maybe even more, to give way to the happiness of the person you love."
- "I think we dream so we don't have to be apart for so long."
- "If we're in each other's dreams, we can be together all the time."
- "If there ever comes a day when we can't be together, keep me in your hearts—I'll stay there forever."

And, of course, the quote that inspired the event: "Nobody can be uncheered with a balloon."

Each person then writes a short note to Elizabeth and attaches the message to a balloon. We move out to an open area, free of trees, and after a countdown, we all release the balloons at the same time. The gentle breeze quickly lifts and wafts them away into the distance.

Kellee has taken video and pictures. I text them to Katherine hoping she will have the same response I had from Lynette's text: *Come back to us, Katherine. This group of women accepts everyone. Your trage-dy doesn't make you less a part of us. We have a seat saved for you.*

Although my son was never mentioned and most people there had no idea of my loss, I felt honored to be a part of this homage to grief. Everything inside me stands and salutes.

This small act of kindness is returned many times over by Katherine. We go to lunch and she tells me all about her life and Elizabeth's life. On Mother's Day she gifts me a poem that Darcy, her sister, wrote. She watches for me each Sunday and we have a brief acknowledgment of shared sorrow.

It's amazing how often grief is connecting. People I had never previously thought of as friends have stepped forward to associate with me. There just isn't a better way to feel comforted than to know that someone is in this with you. In truth, we are all balancing on some edge and wishing for that welcoming nod and wave of inclusion that says, "Come with me—I know the way through this."

Day 671: The Gift of Discarding Soul Clutter

I watch my first episode of Marie Kondo. I'm fascinated with her holistic approach to cleaning and organizing. She suggests taking each article in your home and asking, "Does this spark joy?" If not, discard it. Keep only the things that bring joy. She thanks each item for the service it has given to her.

Although the methods seem simplistic, I can't stop watching. A feeling of great kindness and love wells up inside of me. Her gift is to help clients who are overburdened with clutter work their way through the mess to an orderly, joyful life.

There is so much to be overburdened with during grief—so much clutter floating in and out of your mind. Instead of pushing it down or away, I need to examine it, consider the service it might have rendered to me, and then discard it. Some of these burdens, though seemingly painful or useless, actually spark joy for me. They carry a legacy and a sentimental value that will never be recognized by others. But others have passed their expiration date. It's time to let them go.

Marie Kondo does not clean the house for her clients; she merely gives them the method for doing so. She wants them to know that tidiness has always been within their power; therefore, they can do it anytime in the future as well.

God offers me the same experience. What I choose to think about and ruminate on is always within my power. I can discard what does not serve me well and keep those moments that spark joy. Like tidiness, it's a continual task.

Day 700: The Gift of Temple Perspectives

TRUDI INVITES ME TO GO TO THE TEMPLE WITH HER. I HAVEN'T GONE in a very long time, which may be surprising to most people who know me. But the temple always brings my emotions to the surface— it's a public place, and I don't want to risk falling apart there. I know most of the people who work there, and I don't want the added pressure of trying to soothe their worries. Perhaps that doesn't make sense to anyone else, but to me, it's necessary self-care.

But since it's Trudi, I agree to go. It doesn't seem wise, but I guess I'm a long way past wise in most of my social risks. We sit through the session. Nothing in particular strikes me. When we are in the celestial room, we sit on the couch and begin to talk. Looking back, I'm surprised that no one asks us to leave or to talk more quietly. Perhaps it's evident we're discussing eternal matters because no one interferes. We're left in the room for hours—three hours, actually—to talk and talk.

We discuss so many things: deep things, shallow things, selfish things, and selfless things. As we talk, I realize that we have learned so much. We wonder if mourning is a skill learned through practice, like playing the flute, or if it's a gift given to you at birth, like perfect pitch. Either way, we all have to perform this ritual at some point in our lives. We all will mourn something, and whether it's learned by practice or comes as a natural gift, it's a necessary ability. In fact, it's the first requirement of baptism: to mourn with those who mourn (see Mosiah 18:8–10).

Trudi suggests we share some of the things we have learned with others, especially with our Church leaders. I agree that would be enlightening, but I also realize that just from talking with Pam, Trudi, Suzanne, Cassidy, and others that not every mourner has the same needs or desires. That's what makes it tricky for others to mourn with us. I wonder: What are the principles of mourning? Are there universal ways to meet these unique moments?

Even after experiencing death myself, I can't say that I've become especially adept at mourning with others. I'm merely not afraid to do it anymore. I realize that death is a part of all our lives—not something to shun or fear but something to prepare for and accept.

After all of this—after all the experiences and gifts I have received—if pressed, I would say that the most helpful thing to me was simply to pray the prayer that never fails, the one that always works, the one that brings God in chariots of flaming fire to your side: *Thy will be done.*

Even when I could hardly whisper the words, the comfort was immediate. Then I experienced how Resurrection surely must feel to those who have long been buried beneath sorrow or sin or dirt of any kind.

Mourning requires gifts of self, and not everyone has the same gifts to offer or the same capacity to give, but that doesn't matter. What matters is that you offer what you have. Mourners have a responsibility to accept whatever is offered, no matter how inadequate or even offensive it may appear. Somehow gratitude softens and shines up those repurposed gifts and gives them value.[41]

Day 707: The Gift of Supported Change

THE NEXT WEEK, TRUDI AND I MEET WITH CHARLOTTE, THE STAKE Relief Society president, to share with her some of the thoughts we talked about in the temple. Charlotte has been my friend for several

---

41. For more on receiving offered gifts, see Lisa Clark Valentine, "'Yes, and . . .': The Creative Art of Living" (Brigham Young University devotional, July 20, 2021), speeches.byu.edu.

years, and I know her to be a person of deep faith. She has already been a support to me in other matters

Charlotte listens patiently as Trudi relates some experiences she has had. She is attentive and earnestly seeking to understand. Charlotte herself is no stranger to loss; her mother died when she was nine years old, and her father died two years later. Charlotte was an orphan at age eleven.

But as we all begin sharing things, it gets confusing. It's hard to delineate particular things that help everyone during grief. I can see that things that are helpful to me are not helpful to Trudi and vice versa. Charlotte's experience seems divergent too because she was a child, not an adult.

So we go back to the basics. What is mourning? Mourning is a state of transition. A loss has been experienced, and with it, many things must change: daily routines, spiritual moorings, future expectations.

For the mourner, this means agreeing to undergo a transformation. This transformation entails emotional, intellectual, spiritual, financial, and even physical adjustments at a time when the mourner often feels diminished confidence, support, love, and sense of direction. Often core elements of personal identity are deeply affected.

For those who support the mourner, this means looking for ways to help in this transformation. They should realize that there will be no quick solutions or immediately stable changes. Things will go up and down, back and forth. Therefore, walking alongside the mourner for an extended period is paramount, as is offering acceptance and support through listening, inclusion, and love. The exact methods will be distinctive for every mourner.

Perhaps our biggest takeaway is that grief is an accumulation of many things that we wish were otherwise. Each of these things tends to erode our confidence. We begin to wonder if we really are part of a great and marvelous work—or perhaps we don't matter at all. Are we only valuable when we are whole? Once our cracks and chips start to show, do people still recognize the light within us?

People often say to me, "What a difficult time for you." Yes, certainly. But they say it as if it's an anomaly, as if most of the time things have been running quite smoothly in my life. But the reality is—and

Charlotte knows this—that I don't think there has been a time in the last twenty years that I have not been struggling with something. There is always a problem weighing on me, stretching me, pushing back at me. And I'm certain this is the same for everyone else in the world as well. Perhaps grief has its own category of difficulty because it is an irretrievable loss that takes with it some of our aspirations. Plans have to change.

Charlotte has a spiritual gift for seeing the God-honing purpose in every soul-chipping experience. She is one of those people whose faith seems to run on adversity. The greater the mess, the stronger the message. The higher the test, the clearer the testimony. The longer the trial, the sweeter the triumph. She helps me remember that I have endured many trials, and no matter how halting or circular my progress, eventually I get stronger and stauncher.

Adversity is often how we are drawn to change. And it really is true that no matter how slowly or poorly or haltingly we change, God doesn't impatiently roll His eyes; instead, He raises His fist in triumph.[42]

Day 712: The Gift of Introspection

TODAY I SEE THIS ON AN INSTAGRAM POST, AND IT BRINGS ME UP short:

> Boredom is a sign you need mental stimulation.
> Grief is a sign you need divine elevation.
> Isolation is a sign you need social attention.
> Apathy is a sign you need physical motion.
> Make sure you know the difference.

I stop scrolling immediately as my glass prods me to consider this. The irony that I find this *while* scrolling causes me to immediately self-diagnose. I am, in this moment, trying to alleviate my sluggish sadness with social media. Wrong remedy.

---

42. See Anne Lamott, *Plan B: Further Thoughts on Faith* (New York: Riverhead Books, 2006), 46.

I'm feeling bored, miserable, isolated, *and* apathetic. My current actions are aggravating my aches, not alleviating them. I am oppressing myself instead of blessing myself.

This isn't necessarily new knowledge. I have understood this at some level for a long time. But the phrasing of this post gives that smallest shift of perspective—an infinitesimal movement that is the last centimeter before a mind-altering leap.

I move my Instagram off my home page and deeper into my phone storage. I silence the notifications. Just these small acts alone bring a sort of clarity, as if my glass has set upgraded corrective lenses across my vision—a tiny alteration that illuminates and sharpens what seemed hazy or distant before.

Day 731: The Gift of Thorns

TRUDI BRINGS ME A SUCCULENT TODAY. IT'S IN A CUTE LITTLE BUCKet, and I can tell she's spent time on the choice. She has no idea that Pam brought me a cactus two years ago. She thanks me for the presentation I gave the other night at a Relief Society event, all of which flowed from the conversation we had in the temple over a month ago. She is gracious and kind. I can see she is reaching out to me and exploring her own bravery in all of this. Make no mistake—it *is* bravery.

Thus, today I receive my second cactus. Some of you may see this as a pure coincidence that both my friends who have lost sons give me a cactus. I see it as a pure message from God. After all, God also lost His son while He was crowned with thorns.

It brings to mind this teaching:

The Prophet Joseph Smith declared—and he never taught a more comforting doctrine—that the eternal sealings of faithful parents and the divine promises made to them for valiant service in the Cause of Truth, would save not only themselves, but likewise their posterity. Though some of the sheep may wander, the eye of the Shepherd is upon them, and sooner or later they will feel the tentacles of Divine Providence reaching out after them and drawing them back to the fold. Either in this life or the life to come, they will return. They will have to pay their debt to justice; they will suffer for their sins; and may tread a thorny path; but if it leads them at last, like the penitent Prodigal, to a loving and forgiving father's heart and home, the painful experience will not have been in vain. Pray for your careless and disobedient children; hold on to them with your faith. Hope on, trust on, till you see the salvation of God.[43]

Perhaps the phrase "a loving and forgiving father's heart and home" refers to God the Father, but since it's not capitalized, I wonder if it might reference mortal fathers as well—those who hold the priesthood keys that turn hearts to fathers, bind on heaven what has been bound on earth, and seal families together.

I guess all of us tread some kind of thorny path. Maybe that's because if we don't, we miss the point of this existence, which is to be made perfect through the Atonement of Jesus Christ

Remember when Paul begged God three times to remove the thorn from his flesh? God replied, "My grace is sufficient for thee: for my strength is made perfect in weakness" (2 Corinthians 12:9).

My life might seem devoid of pleasure at the moment—a patch of thorny cacti—but it's abounding with divine connection, and the latter brings more purpose and sustenance than the former ever did. His grace is more than sufficient.

Day 812: The Gift of the Creation, the Fall, and the Atonement of Jesus Christ

I INVITE MY FRIEND MAROLYN TO GO WITH ME TO LUNCH TIME Theater at Herberger, a theater in Phoenix. A presenter gives a performance about addiction. She shares an analogy that gets my jagged glass pumping. As well as I can remember it, her analogy was as follows.

---

43. Orson F. Whitney, in Conference Report, Apr. 1929, 110.

Being a mother is like being a sculptor. You begin with this small lump of impressionable clay. You spend every day of your life molding and refining this clay into a beautiful statue. You're always adding clay and tweaking edges and making small indents and smoothing it as you go.

One day you look down and realize the statue has wheels. And suddenly, out of seemingly nowhere, someone pushes your statue down the mountain.

As it careens off the hillside, you start to run. You have no other choice; you must save this precious creation. The statue is tipping and skidding toward a massive cliff. You know it. You can see it. It's very clear to you what's going to happen. You start yelling and calling to people to stop the statue or to help you.

But the statue doesn't stop. People step out of the way. And sometimes you actually get close enough that you can almost slow it down. Or it tips over and you set it right again. But the unstableness causes it to careen down the mountain again.

You run and run and run—for days or weeks or months or even years.

Then one day, you realize something: you are both going to go over that cliff if you don't stop chasing the statue.

Sometimes the statue stops on its own. Sometimes someone else intervenes and stops the statue. Sometimes you reach it and stop it and haul it back out of the hills. But sometimes it goes over the cliff, and you don't get to see what happens to it after that.

Did it survive? Did it land safely? Did someone catch it that you don't know about? And you just hope that the Master Builder knew how to construct statues that can overcome the Fall.

Day 919: The Gift of Gotcha

ALMOST THREE YEARS HAVE PASSED, AND I STILL FEEL AS IF I'M IN some sort of trapeze act. I spend most of the time spinning and tumbling along, and just before plunging, someone's hands will reach out and grasp me. I am pitched back up and passed along. It feels simultaneously fantastic and frightening. Once in a while a thought skitters across my mind: *What will happen if one day no one is at the end of a somersault?* But so far, it's catch and release, spin and grasp.

I'm only allowed to fall so far. I can't go lower. I mean, obviously I could—I have the drive and capability and all the feels to do so, and I am certainly not a skirter. There is just this safety net in the way now and lots of trapezists reaching out for me.

I'm allowed to tumble, but there are limits. "That's far enough," the glass will say as the net cocoons around me. I can go no further than that.

Then I am bounced back—sprung up, really, with no effort from me at all. I rarely have to climb up the ladder, and I end up right back on the platform. I just have to trust the process. I am so accustomed to the reality of this net that I can almost casually meet pain. Like today.

Another person I know has taken his own life. I see it on Facebook: all the speculation, shock, ideas, explanations, warnings—the wonder and worry—mostly from people who are not close to the deceased. Such is the nature of suicide though. It seems to infiltrate the mind, upsetting preconceived ideas, distressing people who didn't even know them. For a brief second, I am suspended in air, fully stunned, and then plunging—straight down.

I don't know how long I'll be falling. Sometimes it feels like hours, but eventually, I know there's that net down there—somewhere. Or maybe there's an unseen acrobat nearby.

I arrive at church, still free-falling. I'm still comprehending my own reaction, and all I want is to have some time alone to realign myself. I want to be home processing this, but here I am instead. There are days when I wish for nothing more than to just unsee and unknow and unexperience what I have seen, known, and experienced.

As the meeting starts, I see that Elder Eilers will be speaking. He's going home soon—in a few weeks, I think. When he starts his talk, even though I'm on the second row and looking right at him, I'm hardly listening to what he's saying. Then I hear, "You might remember that from a talk Sister Rowlan gave about the woman taken in adultery."

In that moment I feel the hands curl round my wrists, and I am jerked out of my dive and swooping up in a perfect arc. I feel the full sensation of "I gotcha."

Elder Eilers is referencing a talk I gave almost two years ago in this ward. I'm absolutely stunned that he would remember it and comment on it. It's hard to describe the breadth and scale of this internal experience or all that it affects. All my own words were being repeated back to me by him: "Jesus is the Way, the Truth, and the Life. He provides all those things for us—if we come unto Him."

There is a lonely plaintive ache inside me, but the smallest ray of light has reached my glass, which now gleams and shimmers in response. I am filled with love for this ward and this experience. I have met so many kind people and worked with truly dedicated and amazing missionaries. This is one of the best times of my life, and I know it. My glass that has been wailing all morning pitches up to the purest note and holds.

Day 932: The Gift of Entertaining Strangers

TODAY IS CHRISTINE'S BIRTHDAY. WHILE SHE'S AT WORK, I GO TO THE grocery store to get a cake. On the way in, I see a young girl standing out front trying to sell something, but I walk by, eyes averted. I don't have time for that today.

I carefully consider every cake in the bakery. I even ask the bakery assistant for his advice. We talk back and forth about things. Everything is light. Everything is easy. It's a sunny day. I am planning a small celebration.

I need candles. I walk across the store, down the aisle, and see the cake accessories. Just like that, I swallow acid. I remember Brieson and Christine taking a cake decorating class together. I think about all the funny moments they had in the class—moments that can never happen again. I realize how much they must miss each other. I feel how much Brieson must miss Christine today. These memories start churning my heart to pulp.

I blink back emotions. Balancing my candles atop the cake, I head to the self-serve line. I scan, bag, and pay. I'm heading back out the door as a different person than when I entered.

The same little girl steps in front of me. "Hi, I'm Sophie. I'm raising money for my choir group. Would you care to donate?"

I actually don't want to donate, and my hands are full, so I start to mutter a "sorry" and push past her. But then I stop . . . because I have learned to listen for it: the silence that drops like a curtain, just before a spotlight swings onto my glass. Something is about to happen.

I set down the cake on the wobbly table and say, "I usually don't have cash, but let me look." I pull out a five-dollar bill and place it in the clear bubble jar.

"That's very kind," her father says.

I slip my purse over my arm and pick up the cake as I reply, "Well, she will have to sing for me when she gets famous."

Her father says, "She'll sing for you right now!"

I assume the girl will demur, and I smile down at her to assure her that it's okay and she doesn't need to sing. But she has already launched into song: "Hope is the thing with feathers . . ."

My jaw drops. This is my all-time favorite poem. I didn't know it was a song! As she sings each line, I mouth the words.

A fragile joy starts to unfurl, and I can't stop staring at her. As she sings, I feel a depth and intensity of life, as if someone is pumping abundance into the air and light all around me. I feel inflated, renewed, generously supplied.

She sings every verse and one stanza twice because she forgets her place. When she finishes, I ask, "Do you know who wrote that?"

She squints up at me and lifts one shoulder in a half shrug. "I can't remember."

"It's by Emily Dickinson. I have over eighty poems memorized, but that's my very favorite one."

She half-smiles and turns away from me, already looking for her next patron.

And there I am, standing in a strip mall parking lot, fully immersed in the mercy of God. It's uncanny how many envoys He has—just waiting for me to walk by so they can deliver a message that they themselves do not recognize as divine communication. I see how easy it is to entertain angels unaware (see Hebrews 13:2).

I fully recognize, in that moment, the tender mercy God has arranged for me today. On the drive home I recite the poem over and over.

> "Hope" is the thing with feathers -
> That perches in the soul -
> And sings the tune without the words -
> And never stops - at all -
>
> And sweetest - in the Gale - is heard -
> And sore must be the storm -
> That could abash the little Bird
> That kept so many warm -
>
> I've heard it in the chillest land -
> And on the strangest Sea -
> Yet - never - in Extremity,
> It asked a crumb - of me.[44]

Day 1266: Records of Judgment

THIS BOOK HAS BEEN DONE FOR WEEKS—EVERY SINGLE WORD WRITten and every page reworked multiple times in an effort to get it close to reality. It still falls frustratingly short. Numerous times throughout this process I have set it aside, shaking my head that I would never really share this with anyone. It's too revealing—too religious.

This entire week I have been reading and rereading, tweaking small parts and lying awake at night wondering if I should really do

---

44. Emily Dickinson, "'Hope' is the thing with feathers," Poetry Foundation, accessed Aug. 21, 2023, https://www.poetryfoundation.org/poems/42889/hope-is-the-thing-with-feathers-314.

this. Some moments it seems so powerfully important that I do it, and other times I feel foolish for thinking this has any purpose beyond my own education. I understand it, *I* have it, so why share it? Everyone is on their own personal journey, so this can't possibly be important to anyone but me.

This morning I was planning to go to tennis, but instead I lie in bed thinking about the Second Coming of Christ. I have been researching signs of the times. Then, for about the thousandth time, this question drops into my mind: *I wonder if anything I do affects Brieson. It seems like it does. It seems there is a link between my actions and his progress.*

I push the thought aside since I have never really found any doctrine that teaches that. Of course, vicarious work is the very foundation of Christianity: that Jesus Christ, through His own works and sacrifice, saved us. And my religion does teach that vicarious works can be done for earthly ordinances, such as baptisms, confirmations, and sealings. It's a weighty doctrine that my actions can give needed help to those who died without these religious rites. I think we might be the only modern religion that prescribes to this doctrine, even though it is taught by Paul as well. But it seems a leap to think that all my actions are linked to Brieson; wouldn't that negate agency or personal accountability?

I send a few texts to family members and friends and then get up. It's still quite early in the morning. While getting dressed after my shower, I have this sudden compelling idea to look up all the scriptures with the word *works* in them. Immediately, I open up my computer and type it in.

The first hit to come up is Doctrine and Covenants 128. As I read it, the Spirit cascades over me so forcefully that I can hardly read through my tears:

You will find recorded in Revelation 20:12—*And I saw the dead, small and great, stand before God; and the books were opened; and another book was opened, which is the book of life; and the dead were judged out of those things which were written in the books, according to their works.*

You will discover in this quotation that the books were opened; and another book was opened, which was the book of life; but the dead were judged out of those things which were written in the books, according to their works; consequently, the books spoken of must be the books which contained the record of their works, and refer to the records which are kept on the earth. And the book which was the book of life is the record which is kept in heaven; the principle agreeing precisely with the doctrine which is commanded you in the revelation contained in the letter which I wrote to you previous to my leaving my place—that in all your recordings it may be recorded in heaven.

Now, the nature of this ordinance consists in the power of the priesthood, by the revelation of Jesus Christ, wherein it is granted that whatsoever you bind on earth shall be bound in heaven, and whatsoever you loose on earth shall be loosed in heaven. Or in other words, taking a different view of the translation, whatsoever you record on earth shall be recorded in heaven, and whatsoever you do not record on earth shall not be recorded in heaven; for out of the books shall your dead be judged, according to their own works, whether they themselves have attended to the ordinances in their own *propria persona*, or by the means of their own agents, according to the ordinance which God has prepared for their salvation from before the foundation of the world, according to the records which they have kept concerning their dead.

It may seem to some to be a very bold doctrine that we talk of—a power which records or binds on earth and binds in heaven. Nevertheless, in all ages of the world, whenever the Lord has given a dispensation of the priesthood to any man by actual revelation, or any set of men, this power has always been given. Hence, whatsoever those men did in authority, in the name of the Lord, and did it truly and faithfully, and kept a proper and faithful record of the same, it became a law on earth and in heaven, and could not be annulled, according to the decrees of the great Jehovah. This is a faithful saying. Who can hear it? . . .

For their salvation is necessary and essential to our salvation, as Paul says concerning the fathers—that they without us cannot be made perfect—neither can we without our dead be made perfect. (Doctrine and Covenants 128:6–9, 15)

My jagged glass cracks wide open, and I feel as if I am standing on the brink of something very deep and wide and vast. *Are all the things I have experienced and all the things that have floated into my life been because of some assignment Brieson has been given?* I don't know. I can't say for sure. But I do know, undoubtedly know, that these experiences must be recorded.[45]

I feel as if I have been handed years of intentional study, or thousands of hours of experience, in one flash of a moment. Literally a flash. One moment I wondered, and the next moment I completely understood, as if I had been born with this knowledge. Clear. Confirmed. Ratified.

Back to Day 0

THE DAY THAT IT HAPPENED, TODD MUNSON, A MURDER SUSPECT, was killed in a high-speed chase.

President Trump issued an ultimatum to Congress to pass the GOP health care bill or else he would leave ObamaCare as it is and work on other issues.

The FBI announced that Tom Brady's stolen Super Bowl jersey, which had been missing since February 5th, was returned to the Patriots.

An iguana scuttled across the courts at the Miami Open tennis tournament in a match between Vesely and Haas. Haas took a selfie with him.

Scottish researchers unveiled a solar-powered skin that makes prosthetic limbs look closer to the real thing.

But I didn't know any of these things because we had become news ourselves—another name added to the growing list of suicides

---

45. Elder Hyrum Smith, while talking to Edward Hunter concerning his son who had passed away, said, "It is pretty strong doctrine, but I believe I will tell it. Your son will act as an angel to you; not your guardian angel, but an auxiliary angel, to assist you in extreme trials" (Andrew Jensen, *Latter-day Saint Biographical Encyclopedia* [Salt Lake City, UT: Western Epics, 1971], 1:229).

between the ages of 14 and 24. "It's an epidemic," one of the firefighters told us.

I hope never to be newsworthy again.

While everyone else was getting ready for dinner, we were watching the first fire truck roll up to our driveway.

For three years, I have done little else but think of Brieson's death. Describing loss is difficult—how it feels to lose a child, how in losing him I lost myself.

I have written hundreds of pages about this experience, about four times as many as are in this book. This has been one of the most intense experiences of my life—unsought, unwanted, but valuable beyond comprehension. I have lost something for which there is no compensation. As long as I am mortal, there will be a space inside of me where nothing else fits. It is a sacred space.

This book has been about mourning Brieson, but I have not shared much about Brieson himself. Although I have known Brieson all his life, I know him even better now. Death seems to invite more openness and sharing from others, and from him, than there ever was during his lifetime.

I already knew he liked math and prime numbers, creative fiction, reading psychology books, studying unusual topics (his range was voracious), cake decorating (or at least taking classes with Christine), graphic design, being in plays, writing stories, teaching math, roller coasters, computer programming, animation, using Excel, perfect pixels, knitting, babysitting his nieces and nephew, clay sculpting, laughing, trips to Washington, DC, all things *Lord of the Rings*, gold leafing, painting, and collecting coins.

What I learned later is that he likes singing Mariah Carey songs, the beach, making videos with friends, writing letters of encouragement to others, helping people, making lembas bread, having *Lord of the Rings* celebrations, and collecting dirt. He took a Book of Mormon class that changed his life, was a poetry writer, had crazy good app idea ("like an app that takes all the photoshopping off of any photo, reverting it back to its raw image"), and thought about spiritual things more than he ever let on.

After his death, I thought it would be the big events that would cause the heartache, but instead it is the slivers of glass that remain—the ones impossible to see—that cause the most pain. No one uses the small melanin plates or glass bowls anymore—apparently that was Brieson. No one talks to me about prime numbers; no one makes the Christmas potpourri mix; no one tells me about astronomy events; no one helps me with my computer glitches; no one cares about the books I read; no one elaborates on my activity ideas; no one goes too far with their jokes; no one leaves half-made rockets lying around; no one plants flowers; no one leaves bacteria samples in the freezer; no one makes hand-forged sunglass prototypes in the garage; no one bakes Saltine crackers from scratch; no one plays the violin; no one creates unique packaging ideas; no one tells me my pictures are too pixelated and that I need more white space.

I wish he had been with me when I watched Conan's dreadlocks episode and his adoptive Japanese family adventures; when Siearra took me to that cute little bistro for lunch; when I got those teacups from China in the perfect packaging; when the Holocaust speaker came. I wish he would have met Patsy; done the axe-throwing; helped me outdo the absurdity video. He would have loved the e-bikes and the births of Ridge, Rivyr, Kayak, Heath, Summit, and Valli—the nieces and nephews born after he died.

I don't know why he took his life. I'm not sure even he could have articulated it. I assume it was an overwhelming feeling of despair with demons cheering him on, his ruin being their satisfaction.

When Brieson was a little boy, he had a great fear of monsters. My job, as his parent, was to assure him there were no monsters, only shadows—just his imagination. Jacob tells us that delivering us from monsters is one of Christ's missions:

> O how great the goodness of our God, who prepareth a way for our escape from the grasp of this awful monster; yea, that monster, death and hell, which I call the death of the body, and also the death of the spirit. For the atonement satisfieth the demands of his justice upon all those who have not the law given to them, that they are delivered from that awful monster, death and hell, and the devil, and the lake of fire and brimstone, which is endless torment;

and they are restored to that God who gave them breath, which is the Holy One of Israel. (2 Nephi 9:10)

I once believed these monsters were metaphorical, but not anymore. My glass nudges me, always a precursor to alert me that I am missing an expansive lesson. Something falls into place—something elemental. It's such basic Christian doctrine that it cannot be denied or rejected—the very essence of fact: that as harsh and trying as Brieson's experience might be, his deliverance and restoration will exceed it.

All Things Work Together for Good

ABOUT A DECADE AGO, I READ SOMETHING THAT STRUCK A CHORD with me. I wrote it down and sent it to Pam when Ryan died. Perhaps it was a little too soon after his death—these things take time to settle into your soul. I have read this analogy dozens of times in my life and offer it to you as a truth that I have now experienced:

Perhaps the greatest test is whether we, who are Christ's followers, believe the truth of this verse: "And we know that all things work together for good to them that love God, to them who are called according to his purpose" (Romans 8:28).

We should identify the very worst things that have ever happened to us, then ask whether we believe God will in the end somehow use those things for our good. The Bible is emphatic that He will. We have no reason to think He will be any less trustworthy concerning this than with any other promise He has made. Notice that the verse doesn't say that each thing we experience is good in itself, or works for good on its own, but rather that God causes them all to work together for our good, under his sovereign hand. In other words, Romans 8:28 declares a cumulative and ultimate good, not an individual or immediate good.

Before my mother made a cake, she used to set each of the ingredients on the kitchen counter. One day, I decided to experiment. I tasted all the individual ingredients for a chocolate cake. Baking powder. Baking soda. Raw eggs. Vanilla extract. I discovered that almost everything that goes into a cake tastes terrible by itself. But a remarkable metamorphosis took place when my mother mixed those ingredients in the right amounts and baked them together.

The cake tasted delicious.

In a similar way, each trial and apparent tragedy tastes bitter to us. Romans 8:28 doesn't tell me "it is good" if my leg breaks or my house burns down, or I am robbed and beaten, or my child dies. Rather, God carefully measures out and mixes all the ingredients together, including the most bitter ones, and in the end, as measured after life here is done, produced a wonderful final product. Paul goes on in Romans 8 to explain the basis on which he can claim that God works everything together for our good: "For those God foreknew he also predestined to be conformed to the likeness of his Son" (Romans 8:29).

Although we may define our good in terms of what brings us health and happiness now, God defines it in terms of what makes us more like Jesus. If God answered all our prayers to be delivered from evil and suffering, then He would be delivering us from Christlikeness. Despite all appearances, God can redeem the most terrible situations.

If Romans 8:28 means anything, surely it means that.[46]

Now, having suffered a magnificent loss of my own, I believe these words of Paul even more today than I did then. I can testify that God's love never left me. He was always within easy distance. In the long run, we need truth more than we need sympathy. And nothing awakens your senses to reality faster than loss.

As with all experiences, this was not exactly what I imagined it would be. I discovered there is a spectrum of awareness between the black and white of mourning and rejoicing. Sometimes falling and losing reveal more than you imagined you had in you.

Perhaps I have said all this as if things were easily acted upon. The decisions were clear—no shadows or doubts, just pure black and white. But there was a great deal of weighing of things one against another. Each decision came at some cost.

In the beginning I thought, *I will never forget any of this.* But sometimes *never* is less time than you think. These were powerful

46. Randy Alcorn, *The Goodness of God: Assurance of Purpose in the Midst of Suffering* (Colorado Springs, CO: Multnomah, 2010), 97–98.

healing moments, life-changing and saving experiences, but if I would not have written them down, I would have forgotten almost all of them. Most only happened in a second, difficult to capture and point to, like throwing a rock in a stream to mark the spot.

There was a kind of holiness to these days, painful as they were—they always had an otherworldly quality about them that now is beginning to slip away from me. There are days when I feel that I am almost coming back into myself. That is not the happy thought you might think it is. In some ways I never want to leave this euphoric state of divine attention, but already it's losing its hold on me. I can feel God nudging me out of the nest.

That's because God wants me to come back into this world and provide witness to all of His many ministrations. I hope I have done so. I hope you can see that God was part of every tiny kindness and every healing moment. I could see and feel it so clearly.

If I had to name one thing that provided this sight, I think it would be gratitude. I know that sounds so contradictory in my situation, but I cannot deny that it always seemed like the more grateful I was, the more God sent people to me.

I hope you understand that grief makes so many things seem damaged and ruined. Grief affects many dimensions; it is not just sadness. My heart did break that day, into a thousand little shards, but God is growing it back again. It's wiser, kinder, and with greater range than it had before—a range that goes beyond the veil.

Day 778: Black Lights and Stained Glass Windows

TONIGHT WE WENT ON A SCORPION HUNT AT LAKE PLEASANT. WE took Patsy (age 9) and Elania (age 11) along with us—two girls from the ward we were assigned to serve in. The guide tried to caution us that because of the cooler weather, we may not see many scorpions—"it's just too cold." And with this thought in mind, he marches ahead of the column of novices. We have hardly gone one hundred yards when Patsy yells, "I see something!"

The forest guide—carrying authority and experience and knowledge—trundles back to check. Patsy hadn't just found one scorpion; she had found several. They were in a bush on the side of the trail—one that the guide and a dozen people passed, shining their black lights on but not really looking because the expert's example had signaled there was nothing of value there.

But several yards back, scouring the landscape, was the real scorpion hunter. With the unsophisticated eye of a child, Patsy saw them. Perhaps her height gave her a different perspective and allowed the proper angle from her flashlight beam. We ended up finding several dozen scorpions that night—all three varieties: bark, giant hairy, and stripetail. Each discovery was a surprising curiosity.

Anyone could have traversed that entire trail—up and down, back and forth, with a high-intensity flashlight—and been completely unaware there were any scorpions at all. In the normal flashlight beam they are completely camouflaged, but with the black light they are illuminated in the most wondrous way. They glow and seem almost ghostly in appearance, yet they are real, completely sentient, and abundant.

Sometimes, through all of this tragedy and all of this loss, I have wanted to stop and yell, "I see something!" Things that others, even experts, seem to brush by with hardly a glance become fluorescent with glowing iridescence. I usually don't point them out because it jars people. These aren't topics we discuss openly in this world. I even told several people, "There have been so many miracles with this experience," but not a single person asked me what they were. And I wonder why. Why don't we allow black lights to illuminate more things for us?

After five years, I still can't tell you why this tragedy occurred. But I do know that in some sort of heavenly transaction, it became a source of both insight and bravery. This jagged-glass experience anchored my soul and changed my wavelength. I became a black light.

The people in these pages may be completely puzzled by what I have related. I fully realize that most people still operate on a non-UV wavelength. It's difficult to believe in the unknown when your life is still familiar—still seems in your control. But I can assure you, having spent years in the black light, that there are things real and abundant all around us—breathtakingly glowing to me but apparently camouflaged to many others.

The underlying premise of this book is that to truly honor the mourning process, we must acknowledge all that loss reveals. It is not just a black hole; it is also a black light. Let us recognize that loss brings a new set of eyes—a new focus on life. Even broken things can teach.

The process continues. Every little piece of broken glass is being picked up, polished, and pieced together. Collectively these fragments are creating a stained-glass structure within me. I realize its purpose is not to satisfy an outside audience but to allow God to shine His light through these shards, beautifying my interior, my outlook, my worship. It functions to provide an illuminating narrative for my life as well as a protection from future storms. And like all works of art, painstakingly brought to fruition, only I will ever know the full cost of its creation.

About the Author

SHELLY ROWLAN WAS RAISED ON A SMALL FARM IN HEBER CITY, Utah. She has a graduate degree in applied ethics but considers applied doctrine to be the most significant educational experience of her life. Shelly believes the greatest thing you can do in this life is to find your gift and then give it away. She currently resides in Phoenix, Arizona, where she and her husband of thirty-nine years raised their five children. *Living with Broken Glass* is her first book.

Scan to visit

https://www.giftsofgrief.org/